Becoming a

Product
Designer

Other Titles in the Series

BECOMING A GRAPHIC DESIGNER, SECOND EDITION
  Steven Heller & Teresa Fernandes

BECOMING AN INTERIOR DESIGNER
  Christine Piotrowski

A GUIDE TO CAREERS IN DESIGN

Becoming a
Product
Designer

Bruce Hannah

WILEY

JOHN WILEY & SONS, INC.

Library of Congress Cataloging-in-Publication Data:

Hannah, Bruce.
Becoming a product designer : a guide to careers in design / by Bruce Hannah.
    p. cm.
ISBN 0-471-22353-0 (Paper)
1. Design, Industrial—Vocational guidance. I. Title.
TS171.H345 2003
745.2'023—dc21
                2003014587

Printed in the United States of America

10 9 8 7 6 5 4 3 2 1

To Elizabeth, Christian, Rebekah,

and most of all

Tanya

Contents

Preface   ix

Acknowledgments   xi

Introduction
Theater of Life   1

Quotes: "What Is Product
Design?"   3

Chapter One
Design Education: What It Is and
What It Isn't   5

Chapter Two
Lighting   47

Chapter Three
Medical   61

Chapter Four
Consumer Products: Everyday
Design   77

Chapter Five
Furniture   115

Chapter Six
Fashion   141

Chapter Seven
Tabletop: Putting Food on the
Table 159

Quotes: "Where Do You Get
Your Ideas?"   169

Chapter Eight
Exhibit Design   171

Chapter Nine
Corporate Design 195

Chapter Ten
The Future of Design 215

Chapter Eleven
Design Entrepreneurs 239

Portfolio 263

Internships 265

Quotes: "Who Are Your Heroes?" 267

Appendix A
Schools Offering Degrees in Product Design 269

Appendix B
Design Organizations 273

Index of Designers 275

Preface

I DIDN'T KNOW that product design existed as a profession until my sophomore year of college, when Lenny Bacich said he was going take it as a major. I asked him what it was and he replied, "Making things." I still think that's a pretty good definition. I loved building stuff as a kid and was lucky to have a locker next to Lenny.

Ask any product designer what he or she does, and usually the reply will be a version of "I make things." Product designers love to make stuff. It really doesn't matter what kind. They love building models, sketching, and mocking up. It's fun to see other peoples' reactions to what you make. It's exciting to build stuff and work out the problems as the form takes shape. Product design is the process of how stuff gets made. Product designers love to dream about what might be, what could be, and maybe what can't be made. Some product designers just draw stuff about the future. Some product designers solve everyday problems. All of it, in the end, makes our lives richer, easier, safer, and more enjoyable.

While interviewing Davin Stowell of Smart Design, I asked him who his heroes were; he replied, "Charles Eames." I told him Charles Eames wasn't a product designer, and he replied, "Everything is product design. Eames designed furniture, exhibits, graphics—just about everything—and it's all product design."

Product design is simply the design of everything we use, from toothbrushes to the computer to the chair you are sitting in. Its breadth is the confusing part, but also what makes it exciting. Product designers create the items we live with, work on, talk into, listen to, ride in or on, write with, and play with. A product designer has been involved in forming just about any activity you can think of, even including exhibitions and thrill rides.

As a profession, product design is relatively new, coming of age only in the last century. Its founders were architects, scenic designers, engineers, and interior designers. Product design isn't engineering; it is the creation of the objects that deliver the engineering and science. Alexander Graham Bell invented the telephone, but product designer Henry Dreyfuss gave the modern phone its form.

As the field developed, educators created courses and entire programs devoted to it. In 1932 Carnegie Technical Institute (now Carnegie Mellon University) started the first program in product design education in the United States. Pratt Institute soon followed. Walter Gropius's Bauhaus in Europe tried to bring together the disciplines of craft, art, and design, thus generating some of the earliest interest in this new art form.

What is product design? If it isn't engineering, what is it? It's taking all that's new and packaging it so that the consumer understands how to use it—or not. It's developing new products with new materials. The iMac, packaged by the product designer Jonathan Ives, is a perfect example of product design packaging. He gave us a vision of what a new computer could be.

Product design is a team sport. Working with engineers, programmers, and marketing specialists, product designers create the physical form of products. They work for corporations (General Motors employs hundreds of designers), in large design offices (IDEO employs 100 designers worldwide), or are freelancers.

Becoming a Product Designer is unique because its core comprises interviews with working product designers, all of whom define their wide-ranging profession a bit differently. Maybe product design is not definable. The people who founded the profession weren't product designers; they were set designers, architects, furniture designers, salespeople, and engineers. Product design can be confusing to define because it is such a hybrid. It's also confusing because its practitioners rarely confine themselves to designing a single type of product. Richard Sapper, the director of design for IBM, has designed chairs for Knoll, Inc., accessories for Alessi, the iconic Tizio lamp for Artemide, and computers. What do you call him—a lighting designer, a furniture designer, or a product designer? He is known as a world-class product designer, a designer for industry.

Teaching product design is a challenge I accepted twenty-five years ago. Finding texts to incorporate into classes has always been a challenge. The texts are based on either architecture or art—or, worse, they are technical books that read like engineering texts. Product design's roots are in architecture, art, and engineering, but it's much more than the sum of these parts.

Teaching design incorporates aspects of other disciplines, but the resulting technical understanding is combined with formal expression. Most schools teach product design as a heavily researched formal expression, which is kind of what it is, but not really. Product design is really about making stuff—that is, transforming information about a problem, relayed by the consumer, the manufacturer, the engineer, the salesman, the marketer, and the client, into a solution that satisfies everyone. Product designers are modern-day alchemists who work to turn dirt into gold. In the eyes of the product designer, this difficult task is worth the effort.

Philosophically, I try to teach my students to be good listeners and makers. Product designers draw, manipulate computers, sculpt, build models, and, with myriad other skills, communicate their three-dimensional ideas to the world. Product design is a performing art. Many designers think of their products as gifts—gifts that perform functions and at the same time are beautiful. Any designer will tell you that creating a product is the best experience anyone could have. Making things is what it's all about. *Becoming a Product Designer* tells that story in as many different ways as products get made.

Acknowledgments

I would like to thank all the contributors who made this book possible; without their insights, thoughtful replies, and work there would be no story. I would also like to thank Margaret Cummins, my editor at John Wiley & Sons, for believing there was a book about product design worth writing, and Rosanne Koneval, assistant editor, for her untiring dedication to this project and her editorial choices.

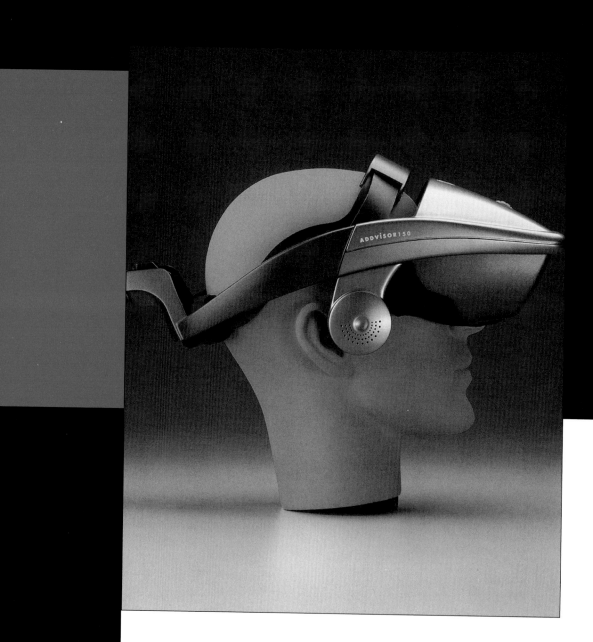

Theater of Life

While walking through an exhibition of Russel Wright's designs at the National Design Museum I was struck by the difference in intent between architecture and product design. It was an early drawing of a theater set by Wright that made it clear that product designers create products for the theater of life. Architects at this time were still immersed in formality of design, concentrating on environments that demanded a certain formal way of life. Many of the early product designers came from the theater, and their training was in creating illusions for the theater—sets and props. If you think about it, it's a logical extension to design props and sets for the theater of life. Mary and Russel Wright's *Guide to Easier Living*, published by Simon and Schuster in 1950, is a book filled with illustrations about how to entertain. The Wrights were reacting to the new lifestyle and modern living. Their products were created to fill the needs of this new lifestyle, which was less formal, more relaxed, and easier.

Other product designers were also responding to the new informality. Eva Zeisel, with her Town & Country earthenware for Red Wing Pottery in 1947 and her Museum line for the Castleton China Company, influenced the way of life that was developing; designed so colors could be mixed and matched, these lines started to break down the barriers between design and the consumer, allowing consumers the opportunity to create their own visions of what their table could look like. The forms also took on a playful attitude that invited curiosity and instilled humor into everyday life. This was a giant step away from the rigid formality of Sunday dinner with the in-laws.

Supporting the theater of life became the job of the product designer, who created products that were easier to use, safer, and more comfortable than earlier designs. Understanding, helping define, and supporting the rituals of daily living is what a product designer does. The theater of life is filled with acts, actors, and actions that drive designers to create better and more interesting products. Designers fill this book with their observations of daily life. Almost all are people-watchers at heart; they derive endless joy from watching what people do and figuring out why. Whether they design simple kitchen utensils or complicated medical devices, designers will tell you that watching people perform the tasks of daily life is what leads them to design discoveries that, once made, are incredibly obvious.

"What Is Product Design?"

Product design is the development of new ideas to make products easier to use, more appealing to the eye, and more efficient to manufacture.
—Paul Metaxatos, Proteus Design

The seamless fusion of how a product works with how it looks.
—Joel Delman, 20-20 Design

What product means is constantly changing. But for me it is the process of rendering a thing (solution) utilizing the resources of others (manufacturer/client) to provide some benefit to someone (user).
—Tad Toulis, Motorola

Currently, I would describe it as the design of products, systems, and experiences that make the lives of the users more productive, healthy, and happy. If you compare that definition to Henry Dreyfuss's answer to a similar question in the 1950s, it's pretty much the same.
—Ron Kemnitzer, Kemnitzer Design

Product design does not begin with a sketch. For me, it begins with identifying a need. The need must be real, not some imaginary problem that someone else might have. I cannot think of *product* without thinking of *marketing*. If I cannot figure out how to market it, I abandon the idea early on. Then I consider appropriate technology, testing, the usual things we all do, etc. I fuss with it until the end. When it is all done, the solution should continue the tradition of "doing more with less."
—Craig Vetter, Vetter Design

Basically, industrial design is the profession that designs products—but we do more. But industrial design in the future is going to be less about just making products and more about facilitating the communication between the user and the producer. In other words, we are talented translators.
—Tucker Viemeister, Springtime

Product design is the conception and creation of the tools of everyday living.
—Patricia Moore

I would define product design as the assignment of form to a manufactured product. This assignment is the designer's interpretation of goals and parameters set by the client and respective of the environment.
—Trevor Combs, Super Innovative Concepts

To me, product design is the process of identifying, defining, solving, inventing, and shaping physical solutions to the problems of living.
—Peter Bressler, Bressler Group

To me, product design is the whole design line—going from beginning to end when designing and developing products. Doing it a lot and doing it for a whole lot of different products, processes, materials, and so on.
—André Grasso, Index Industrial Design

Giving form, reason, and personality to the inanimate.
—George Schmidt, George Schmidt Design

Chapter One

Design Education: What It Is and What It Isn't

The visual arts comprise the only area of endeavor I can think of where you are judged on what you produce much more than on who you are. So deciding to pursue an education in product design means, first, that you are confident in who you are as a person. Once you have decided to pursue a dream of designing products, making a good choice about where to study is the most important decision you will face. Are you a city person or country person? Do you want to study in a big school or small school? All of the choices you make offer advantages and disadvantages. You know yourself and must make those decisions in an informed way. Product design education is as varied as the field. Some schools specialize in designing automobiles, some in user-centered design. You have to find your fit. What is true about all design schools is that they are looking for students with analytical minds who have an interest in the arts. If you are interested in building things but architecture seems too big or too distant, then product design may be for you. Being inventive and curious about how stuff gets made are also indicators that product design is your field. Product design education is not engineering, but product designers work with engineers. A natural curiosity about the world will also serve you well in design school.

Foundation Year

So what is design school like? If you are lucky enough to have attended a high school with design classes, you probably have a pretty good idea what design school is like. If not, you may wonder why no one ever told you such places exist.

Most design school programs last four years, of which the first is a foundation year. In this year you explore various areas of design while taking classes in drawing, three-dimensional design, color, computer-aided design, and academic courses such as history, writing, and psychology. Some schools concentrate on narrow areas of design throughout the four-year course of study, but you will probably have the opportunity to take studio classes in exhibit design, product design, transportation design, and tabletop design. Also, many schools offer related classes such as glassblowing, woodworking, and foundry. Design schools are often part of a larger art school or architecture school; these present many more opportunities to explore additional areas of study. The foundation year lets you experience many areas of design, which helps you decide whether or not product design is really what you want.

After the foundation year, if you choose to continue in product design, the courses get more finely tuned in terms of process and execution of the designs. Most schools require you to take a variety of studio courses, from transportation to exhibit design. This allows you and the school to assess your strengths and weaknesses, to discover where you fit in this varied field.

Teachers

Most design school faculty members are working design professionals who teach once or twice a week. This is a great way to get an education because such professionals bring the real world into the classroom. Students are exposed to the latest thinking and most advanced practices.

Sketching

Being able to sketch ideas quickly and understandably is a big part of how designers communicate with each other and clients. This doesn't mean you have to draw beautifully, but you do need to learn to draw as a means of describing an idea quickly and efficiently. You will find that the people who are good at drawing trees may not be as good at drawing ideas. Sketching can be taught, so don't worry if you're not Leonardo da Vinci with a pencil. Remember, you probably drew pictures before you learned to write.

Models

In design school, you will learn to make models of products and ideas. The more skilled you become at quickly creating a model, the more easily people will understand what you are talking about. Design school teaches you to communicate ideas quickly and clearly in any medium—sketching, modeling, or computer-aided design. You will learn to produce models that describe exactly what you have in mind.

Problem Solving

Design schools teach students how to observe, research, and understand the problems people have either using or manipulating a product. This, at first, seems like it must be easy—but it isn't. Students can stubbornly resist believing that other people actually exist in the world, let alone that they actually have real problems.

Design school isn't technical school, although it may have "Institute" in the name. This is probably a holdover from the founder's need to educate workers. Don't be distracted by the name of a school; most are art-driven and home to many fine teachers.

Computers

All design schools emphasize the use of computers. Being able to execute design on the computer makes it easier to get most jobs done, so take as many computer design classes as possible. On the other hand, the computer is, as you have probably been told, just a tool. IT (Information Technology) is only one way designers communicate ideas.

Corporate-Sponsored Projects

Another component of design education today is corporate-sponsored design research projects. Most schools in the third- or fourth-year design studios introduce students to the world of corporate design. Projects range from pure research to actual design experiences.

Materials and Processes

Understanding how things get made is a big component of a product design education. This is where your curiosity about the world can help. The greatest idea in the world is nothing if it can't be made. This is also where product design starts to veer off from art. Art is usually a one-of-a-kind piece, whereas product design is about making tens of thousands, if not millions, of one thing. Visiting factories and learning how products are actually made should interest you; if it does not, you are definitely in the wrong field. Product designers revel in the making of stuff.

Social Responsibility

One area of design is devoted to research into socially responsible components of design. Two aspects of this area, among many, are *universal design*, which is the design of products usable by people with a range of physical abilities, and *sustainable design*, which addresses recycling and the effect product design has on the environment.

Studios

Many industrial design programs provide studio space for their students. A few years ago, this was a luxury most schools couldn't afford, but it is much more common now. The big advantage to both the school and the student is the learning that goes on between students when these facilities exist. Studios provide a home base for teachers. In some schools, students move each semester from one studio to the next. The advantage to students is they are constantly challenged by new groups of students.

Graduate Programs

Until recently, few graduate product design programs existed; now most design schools have them. The most interesting thing about graduate design schools is that some do not require an undergraduate degree in design—so if your background isn't in design, there is still a good chance you can study it at the graduate level. Most programs last two years, but that can stretch to three if you require remedial training. All graduate programs are research-oriented, and students spend at least two semesters writing and producing a thesis. Again, in some of the schools you will discover your strengths and weaknesses and exactly where you fit in the design world. Not everyone ends up a designer, but the design field includes many types of work. If teaching is in your future, a graduate degree is becoming a must.

You can find a list of schools that offer degrees in industrial and product design in Appendix A.

School: Pratt Institute

EDUCATOR: PETER BARNA
Title: Professor of Art and Design
Program Name: Department of Industrial Design
Location: Brooklyn, New York

What is SPAN?
SPAN is a not-for-profit design company located at Pratt Institute, which was originally funded in 1997 by the Alfred P. Sloan Foundation. SPAN has both an educational mission and a community mission to support small businesses. It provides opportunities for students to work in a semiprofessional environment on real projects with real clients. And it provides design services in the New York City area for small- to medium-sized businesses that would not typically use a designer.

Is it like an internship for students?
It's like an internship except that the students' investment is greater because the firm relies on them to do the design work and interface with the clients.

Who are SPAN's clients?
They are community-based merchants in the SPAN neighborhood. Initially we did a lot of work on websites during the Internet craze.

Product: Net Name Licensing Logo
Designer: Eben Burr
Creative Director: Peter Barna
Design company: SPAN
Client: Net Name Licensing.com, Inc., Richard Blank, CEO; Howard Fleischer, President
Year: 1999

What's your favorite design that SPAN has done?
That's a tough call because the designs are so different. I did enjoy the process of working with a start-up Internet company. During the initial planning we helped form and clarify for them what the company was about and what role design would play in the organization. We worked from the ground up, when nothing existed, to create identity, tools, collateral material for sales, a website. The design felt complete, and the students got to see how a dream becomes a reality.

Product: Duncan's Fish Market
Designer: Patricia Slee, Jonas Concepcion, Juan Castillo
Creative Director: Peter Barna
Design company: SPAN
Client: Myrtle Avenue Revitalization Project, Jennifer Gerend, Executive Director
Year: 2000

What's the most successful project?

A local merchant who had run a fish market for twenty years had to move because his landlord doubled his rent. After finding a space with better rent in a slightly less desirable location, he was willing to take a chance that design could improve his business. We worked closely with him to understand who his clients were and how his store worked. We produced an upscale design that's usually not found in this working-class, predominantly African American neighborhood. His success has been phenomenal. He is selling exactly the same product, but the business doubled literally overnight. In one year he has been able to pay off all his capital investment and is now in a position to buy the building.

Because we get work-study money designated for community service, the designs people get are of high quality without the cost. We're able to show that the small investment in design makes the difference.

What are some other projects SPAN has designed?

We help very small, local businesses gain entrée into national and international markets they normally couldn't get into. One client is a small-scale, Brooklyn-based, family-operated manufacturer of gift-with-purchase giveaway bags. This company couldn't get in the door of some major players. They realized they were perceived as a low-cost manufacturer because they didn't add value to their product. We positioned them to go to potential clients and show "what-if ideas" and other capabilities besides just manufacturing so they can partner with marketing companies to develop products. Now they're packaging items for Swiss Army.

Has SPAN redesigned a block of stores on Myrtle Avenue?

That project was to visually document an existing block and then create proposals of what it could become—basic streetscape design. We digitally documented the buildings and made minimal changes we thought could happen: adding trees, replacing existing streetlights with historic lights, and adding new awnings and graphics to present the businesses better. We got a grant to do the improvements.

We do a wide range of projects. We're a shopping center for design services, which is especially important to small manufacturers who may need some graphics—menus or business cards—a little interior design work, updating a website. Buying that range of design services usually meant dealing with a large design company. We employ students and faculty from a variety of departments, depending on the client's needs.

Product: Myrtle Avenue (after)
Designers: Patricia Slee, Jonas Concepcion, Juan Castillo
Creative Director: Peter Barna
Design company: SPAN
Client: Myrtle Avenue Revitalization Project, Jennifer Gerend, Executive Director
Year: 2000

Product: Swiss Army Packaging Concepts
Designer: Jonas Concepcion
Creative Director: Peter Barna
Design company: SPAN
Client: Premier Pack Industries, Inc.
Year: 2001

What's your dream for SPAN?

The initial dream was to become totally self-sufficient; we charge for everything we do, and everybody gets paid. The dream now is for SPAN to serve as an example to other design schools, which have tended not to take advantage of the talent available in their students and faculty and use them as part of the educational process to contribute to the overall culture. SPAN is a model that other schools can emulate.

Is your work at SPAN still teaching?

It's a schizophrenic situation. On the one hand I'm trying to teach students to dream at the highest aesthetic level, and on the other hand I'm teaching them to deal with the reality of floor drains and building inspections. SPAN plays a part in getting students to understand that even within absolutely beautiful design, if the phone number is spelled wrong on the awning outside the store, that's a problem. That's the difference between art and design: Design has to serve the functional aspects clearly and beyond that what the designer does builds culture.

What is your design philosophy?

Balance! It comes from a personality that is inherently schizophrenic. I'm trying to constantly find the middle ground of who I am between a rural West Virginia upbringing and my life in one of the major cities of the world, between an aesthetic sensibility that runs to the bottom of middle-class America and having aspirations of high art.

What would you design if you could?

I've always dreamed of designing a rubber band that would go about three times the distance of existing ones. I loved to shoot rubber bands when I was a kid in school, and I've done a bit of aerodynamic testing. At some point when I get a little time, I'm going to design a long-flying rubber band.

Product: Waste Match
Designers: Jonas Concepcion, Juan Castillo
Creative Director: Patricia Slee
Design company: ITAC (Industrial & Technology Assistance Corps.)
Year: 2000

School: Fashion Institute of Technology, State University of New York

EDUCATOR: JUDY ELLIS
Title: Chairperson and Founder
Program Name: Toy Design Department
Location: New York City

Why did you start a toy design studio?
This is the first and only one in the country. A toy company asked the Fashion Institute of Technology (FIT) to sponsor a competition, and the college invited me to project-direct it. After the competition, the toy industry asked me if FIT would work with it to develop such a program. I was fortunate to have a fabulous advisory board and to visit the top manufacturers to understand from the top down how the industry worked.

How long is the program?
The program is a two-year bachelor's program in the junior and senior year, with a summer internship and an intense interim experience.

Product: Bug's Playhouse
Designer: I-Ju Lo
Year: 2001

What is the first toy design experience the students have?
In the first semester we expose the students to many categories of toy design—action figures, games, plush toys. The students develop a portfolio of sketches, which is used to obtain an internship. Then they create an ideation book so we can see their design process. (We do that with every assignment during the entire program.) They also design a hard toy, where they make a model and use the shop to create a finished model.

Product: Dinotopia Licensed Product
Designer: Warren Frederick
Year: 2000

All the classes are team-taught with a design component and an engineering component. All students have to learn to do engineering drawings because if a project can't be manufactured, it won't go anywhere. We have student product review meetings once a month so we can figure out what each student needs and counsel them.

In the spring semester, juniors begin developing plush toys based on character development. We talk about values and what the student would like to communicate to a child through the character. The students then do design sketches and create a prototype. Over the summer, the students do a full-time internship, and they are required to keep a notebook and have a daily conversation with their character. They must answer a number of questions and spend at least twenty minutes a day writing and sketching to develop their character. When they come back in the fall, the first thing they do is describe who their character really is. Then they develop the storybook that goes with their character, creating both illustrations and text. Story-telling is critical to toy design because storytelling is critical for the child.

(top to bottom)
Product: My Wonderland Snowball
Designer: Ryo Yoshihara
Year: 2002

Product: Piranha Panic
Designer: Westly Ciaramella
Year: 2000

Product: Dr. Fabulous Game
Designer: Ryo Yoshihara
Year: 2000

(clockwise from top left)
Product: Action figure
Designer: Michael Montalvo
Year: 1991

Product: Character sketches
Designer: Warren Frederick
Year: 2000

Product: Action figure
Designer: Peter Pajillo
Year: 1996

Product: Character sketches
Designer: Warren Frederick
Year: 2000

Product: Character sketches
Designer: Warren Frederick
Year: 2000

Does the character design and development help tie the program together?

Weaving the curriculum together helps take students beyond where they would normally go. Each class builds on the next. For instance, in the licensing course, the students use their character as a way to understand the procedures. Licensing is all about understanding your character.

Do the students get to interact with children?

In one component called Discover Together, students go on nature walks and do other activities with kids, and they work at a day-care center once a week in their first year. While they are creating their character, they are playing with children. That helps them realize how challenging a design must be. We also do focus groups. We invite a school in so the students can learn first-hand how their games play and get reactions to their characters.

Do you try to help students find their strength?

Absolutely! The toy industry is great because it offers so many areas to design in. Some designers enjoy all areas and want to work in an inventors group. Others enjoy various specialties. Some people thrive in the corporate environment, and some are better at family-owned businesses. When students leave here, they have a good sense of direction. We don't clone a style. We work to develop each individual.

What does the toy industry look for in a portfolio?

People in the industry look for both blue sky and reality. They want to see the process, they want to see something unique, and they want to see that it can be manufactured.

(left to right)
Product: Kaleid-o-Camera
Designer: Leslie Barbiero
Year: 2002

Product: Bug's Playhouse
Designer: I-Ju Lo
Year: 2002

Product: Monster Viewer
Designer: Michael Sala
Year: 2002

(left to right)
Product: Dew storybook and plush figure
Designer: Roseld Lagualan
Year: 2002

Product: Cat storybook and plush figure
Designer: Leslie Barbiero
Year: 2002

Product: Shelly So Shy storybook and plush figure
Designer: Toni Gagarin
Year: 2002

Who is your design hero?
Nature—everything comes from nature.

Why did you become a teacher?
To teach is both a privilege and a challenge. Having the opportunity to watch students translate their educational experience into the design of meaningful and valuable products for children gives me a great deal of satisfaction and hope for the future.

How do you teach design?

Team teaching encourages the exchange of ideas, and lively dialog is integral to the lesson. I have worked to shape the curriculum to make sure it is both cumulative and interwoven, the subject of one class reappearing in another, building on existing knowledge. I insist our designers go beyond the classroom to experience the world at large. Designers who reconnect with childhood's sense of magic and discovery are far better able to sense the specific and boundless curiosities in a child's mind.

What qualifications do you look for when accepting design students to your program?

Accepted candidates have excellent abilities in conceptual design and visual communication. We look for people who have innate curiosity, an instinct for discovery, freshness of thought, good values, a good sense of self, and a good sense of humor; they must be energetic, sensitive, committed, and concerned about kids. Our goal is finding mature, focused, responsible, hard-working, exceptional designers who are sensitive to the needs of children and who can succeed in the program and, ultimately, in the industry. We also try to create a group of twenty-one people who will play well together. That's why during our admissions process we consider everyone at the same time.

(left to right)
Product: Mother and baby ducks
Designer: Danielle Parisi
Year: 2002

Product: Spin 'n' Go Octi
Designer: Ronald Laguatan
Year: 2002

Product: Brutus the Brontosaurus
Designer: Toni Gagarin
Year: 2002

What skills do you think are important for students to learn?

Our students learn that the responsibility of the designer is to educate children, providing objects that visually, audibly, and tactilely excite, elevate, inspire, and inform. Designers of children's products are, in essence, designers of information: They select, organize, edit, and present information to children, making a vital and formative impression on them. They must be equipped to answer philosophical questions concerning the purpose and function of toys; they must recognize that the child remains at the center of the product and that technology in toys is most compelling when it engages natural play patterns.

School: Pratt Institute

EDUCATOR: DEBERA JOHNSON

Title: Professor and Chair
Program Name: Department of Industrial Design
Location: Brooklyn, New York

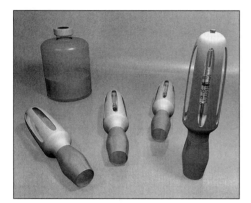

Product: Diabetic syringe
Designers: Tyson Boles and
Jonathan Pettigrew

Product: Diabetic's PDA
Designer: Jaehoon

What's your definition of design?
Design is about imagining the future and being good at deciding how to get there. Designers consider the options and make choices. Good designers are good choosers.

When did you become a teacher?
I became a teacher when one of my Pratt professors, Fred Blumlein, asked me to help him teach his drawing class. I'm not sure why I said yes. I have serious stage fright, and I couldn't sleep the night before class for two years. But something inside said, "Don't give up." That inner voice redirected my career from museum exhibition design to design education. Now I consider myself an education designer: The main material is human. It's fascinating because people don't necessarily stay where you put them or hear or react the same way to things, so it's much harder to predict what's going to work.

What's your most recent design education experience?
Design students need to understand the potential for change that design offers and that design is a vehicle for their individual visual and intellectual talent. I like to explore ways to find solutions to design problems. For example, we recently did an industry project for a large medical company. The project was to design a syringe for people with diabetes. We decided that instead of telling the students what they were designing, we'd gave them the following criteria: "Come up with two- and three-dimensional sketches for a product that is held in the hand that dispenses measured amounts of liquid." The students' sketches included all sorts of materials, and none of them looked

anything like a syringe. We continued to narrow the sketches to final concept in a series of phases, each of which added another layer of functionality and design engineering. I knew we'd really done something substantial when the company's head of marketing remarked, " You know we've been thinking about this stuff for a *long* time, and there are five or six concepts here that have never occurred to us." They had a tough time choosing three finalists, so we presented all twelve to the company's marketing group and research and development (R&D) team. They were impressed by the results and amazed at how the funny, weird sketches had morphed into ingenious solutions. If the students had known at the beginning what they were designing, their concepts would not have been so imaginative.

Product: Furniture design
Designer: Erica Cohen

What qualifications do you look for in prospective students?
The graduate program at Pratt looks for people who have been out of school for a least four years. They are interesting, smart, self-motivated individuals with a good sense of play whose current careers aren't working for them. Their backgrounds are diverse. Choosing students is like inviting good conversationalists to a dinner party. Only the meal they're eating is design.

Product: Toy design
Designer: Wesley Millora

What skills do you think are important?
Foremost is the ability to think and communicate one's ideas. Skills are basic: drawing, model making, researching, planning, speaking, writing, making solid choices, working in teams, and knowing when to bring in the experts.

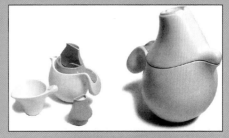

Product: "Cluck, Cluck" tea set
Designer: Peter Valois

Product: Ice skates
Designer: Silas Warren

School: University of Idaho

EDUCATOR: STEVE THURSTON
Title: Professor
Program Name: College of Art and Design,
Architecture, and Interiors
Location: Moscow, Idaho

When did you discover design?
Although I was never very far from art and design in my formative years, it was not until I entered Pratt that the decision to be a designer was consciously and irrevocably made.

When did you become a teacher?
I had given a few lectures and hired interns over many years as a professional designer, and one day I was invited to teach a course. I loved it, eventually becoming a full-time professor. Designing and teaching are inexorably connected by my lifelong absorption with the creative process. Teaching has rejuvenated my own educational process, which in turn rejuvenates my teaching.

What's your most recent design education experience?
Several years ago, I held a studio with some of the very best senior design students at the University of Idaho. We decided to look at transfer chairs and the associated service at airports and on aircraft. I asked a student chair-user, Katie, who had lost the use of one of her arms and both legs, to join our group to help us

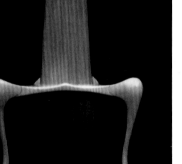

Product: Untitled
Designer: Hugo MacPherson
School: University of Idaho
Description: Cast aluminum and laminated alder. Fabricated by designer. Regional competition winner. Final project for Furniture Design and Construction, a course intended to enhance the ability to think and work in three dimensions with attention to both form and function.

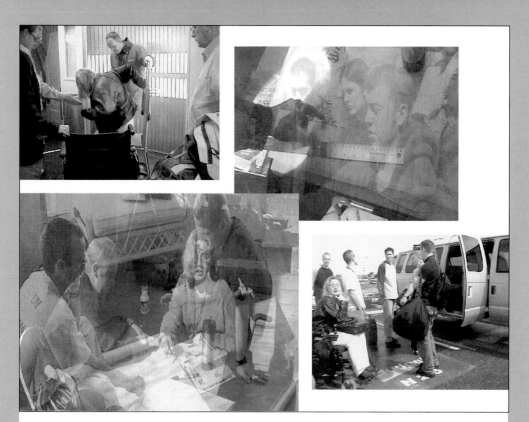

understand the task. She agreed to let us accompany her to San Francisco to visit IDEO. We geared up with plenty of video equipment and mental preparation, expecting to experience ambivalence, infringement of dignity, even physical abuse. However, the airport and airline attendants went out of their way to assist us and to preserve Katie's dignity in every way. The trip seemed to be a success—though we did not encounter much that would help us design a better transfer chair—until the charrette and debriefing. After we divided into small teams using the renowned IDEO open-minded, democratic process, it quickly became obvious that the students had developed strong internal animosities and could not achieve anything. I was baffled until I questioned them individually. The experience had been highly emotional as we got to know Katie and tried to understand her life while sharing the stress of caring for her needs. Some students felt others were not serious enough about the objectives; others thought some were too serious. What had really happened was that Katie's courage and good spirit had made the unchallenged students feel guilty and small. We all learned a great deal in those few days: less about product design than we anticipated, far more about universal design than we imagined.

Product: Transfer chair
Designers: Katie Heimsch, Paul Long, Chad Gerhardt, Suzie Leonard, Erik Fong, Katie Decker, Shad Beazer, Emily Duchek, Ted Mayer, Brian Wickersham
School: University of Idaho
Description: Research project for elective industrial design studio to explore the challenges of air travel by chair users.

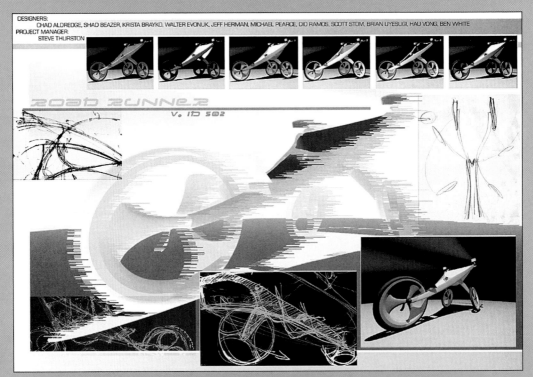

DESIGNERS:
CHAD ALDREDGE, SHAD BEAZER, KRISTA BRAYKO, WALTER EVONUK, JEFF HERMAN, MICHAEL PEARCE, DIO RAMOS, SCOTT STOM, BRIAN UYESUGI, HAU VONG, BEN WHITE
PROJECT MANAGER:
STEVE THURSTON

Product: Baby Jogger
Designers: Chad Alldrege, Shad Beazer, Krista Brayko, Walter Evonuk, Michael Pearce, Jeff Harman, Dio Ramos, Scott Stom, Brian Uyesugi, Hau Vong, Ben White
School: University of Idaho
Description: Baby jogger (presentation for a hypothetical client). Designing primarily through the charrette process, the team considered function, form, materials and market research thoroughly.

What qualifications do you look for in prospective students?

Enthusiasm and open-mindedness. With these and good teaching, a student can go almost anywhere.

What skills do you think are important?

Critical thinking, especially as related to the creative process, and proficiency with technological communication tools are obvious. But experiential learning—feeding the senses voraciously—is also essential. People skills, those humanistic attributes that help us survive and, occasionally, flourish, are indispensable. Students who get to know their professors (mentors) and learn from them through conversation ultimately stand to gain the most from the education process.

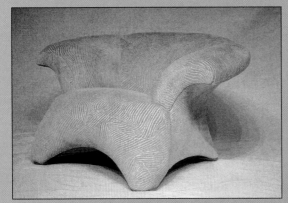

Product: Lounge Chair
Designer: Nicolas Fouch
School: University of Idaho
Description: Upholstery on wood frame. Fabricated by designer. Regional Competition winner. Final project for course entitled Furniture Design and Construction.

School: Carnegie Mellon University

EDUCATOR: CRAIG VOGEL

Title: Professor
Program Name: School of Design,
College of Fine Arts
Location: Pittsburgh, Pennsylvania

When did you discover design? When did you know it was what you wanted to do?
I knew I wanted to be a designer the minute I saw the displays in the industrial design department at Pratt Institute my senior year in college.

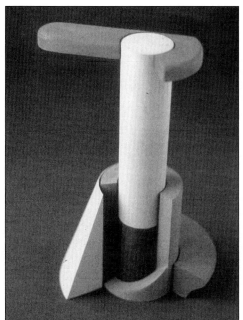

Why did you become a teacher?
When I met Bill Fogler and Rowena Reed Kostellow at Pratt, I knew I was experiencing an area of knowledge and a style of teaching that I could convey to others. It's a gift to inspire others to work in an area that deals with improving the human condition. Designers can help make the world a better experience for human beings by making the products they use more useful, usable, and desirable.

Product: Food Processor
Designer: Madeline Gerstein
School: School of Design, Carnegie Mellon University
Year: 1991
Description: Students develop a set of abstract shapes, combine them into abstract compositions, then decide on product function and refine the form to best suit it.
Photo: Bill Redic

Product: Space and Image
Designer: Unknown
School: School of Design, Carnegie Mellon University
Year: 1999
Description: Foamcore box with spatial design created by juxtaposition of rectangular planes with slides projected into the box. The final piece is the photograph of the assemblage.

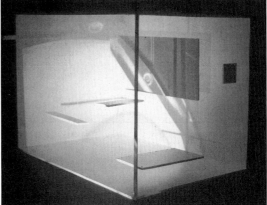

How do you teach design?

I teach design in three ways. I introduce first-year students to the process of visual problem solving through introductory or foundation design. Through design history, I introduce students to the emergence of design as a modern discipline and provide them with a basic literacy. Through the process of interdisciplinary design, I have seniors and graduate students work with students in business and engineering because they need to learn how to work with the other disciplines in the product development process.

Who was your mentor?

I have a mentor on each shoulder. One is Rowena Reed Kostellow, who always reminds me of the need to push students to attain the highest level of visual expression—to place the role of beauty, balance, and visual order over every other factor. The other is Jay Doblin, who challenges me to see the big picture of design as a system of interactive decisions. He pushes me to search for the constants and variables and to look at how design must continually respond to change.

What qualifications do you look for when accepting design students to your program?

I look for students who want to apply their ability to improve the way we live our lives. The difference between art and design is how people apply their ability. Artists can choose their own themes and audience; designers must enjoy exploring the constraints and variables supplied by others. I am interested in students with talent, not students who want to satisfy their own egos. I am also interested in students who want to learn how to verbally articulate their work.

What skills do you think are important for students to learn?

Students need to learn how to develop an idea. But an idea is only the beginning. The real challenge is pushing the idea to its full potential. Students need to see an idea as the beginning of a journey of discovery.

Students also need to understand that people are more important than the product. Learning to understand people is critical to understanding what to design. It is critical to the design process to solve the right problems and to invite the people who will use the product into the process.

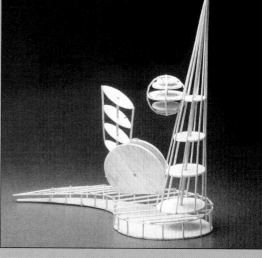

Product: Curvilinear Forms in Dynamic Composition: A Variation Using Open Structural Forms
Designer: Mark McJunkin
School: School of Design, Carnegie Mellon University
Year: 1992
Description: Open-frame structures composed of curvilinear forms placed in dynamic relationship to one another to create the complete composition.
Photo: Bill Redic

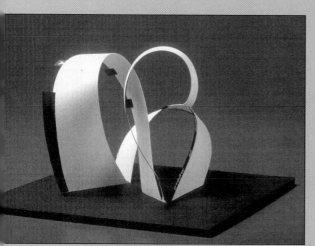

Product: The Balance of Planes and Phrases: The Integration of Words, Surfaces, and Space
Designer: Elizabeth Kleekamp
School: School of Design, Carnegie Mellon University
Year: 1991
Description: Abstract composition using paper planes on cardboard space, showing visual tension between plane surfaces and negative spaces. A phrase is integrated into into the composition, which guides the reader through the phrase.
Photo: Bill Redic

School: Georgia Institute of Technology

EDUCATOR: LORRAINE JUSTICE
Title: Professor and Director
Program Name: Industrial Design Program
Location: Atlanta, Georgia

When did you discover design? When did you know it was what you wanted to do?

I discovered industrial design in my mid-twenties when friends began to talk about how good design could make the world a better place. I was bitten by the design bug and never looked back.

Why did you become a teacher?

Working in industry from the late 1970s through the 1980s, I became disillusioned with the ego-driven design of that era. I kept thinking there must be more, so I decided to get a masters degree at Ohio State University. A professor named Joseph Koncelik taught the graduate students about design research and human-centered design. It was exactly what I was looking for—something of substance, a way to explore and evaluate design solutions. I also realized I had design and computing skills that students needed. I love the academic environment, but I consult to stay current with industry.

How do you teach design?

It's important to teach the students what good design looks and acts like, but it's also important to teach what's not good design and to describe why. One of my favorite studio exercises is asking students to bring in examples of bad design: appliances, tools, and websites, anything that could be improved. Students often feel more confident critiquing something bad, especially at the beginning of a studio. It gets the creative juices flowing.

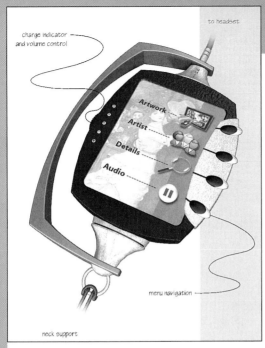

charge indicator
and volume control

to headset

Artwork

Artist

Details

Audio

menu navigation

neck support

Product: Exhibit Floor Plan Art, Active Response Tour Guide
Designer: Michael Dubois
School: Georgia Tech

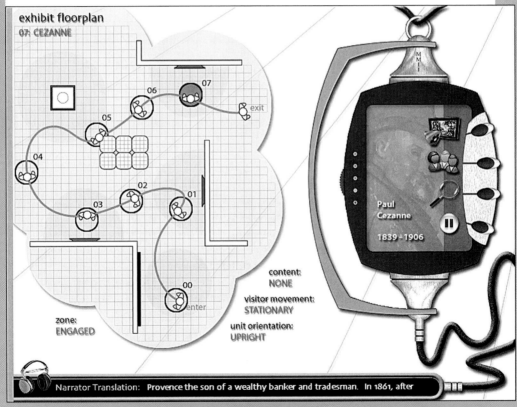

exhibit floorplan
07: CEZANNE

07

06

05

04

03

02

01

00
center

exit

content:
NONE

visitor movement:
STATIONARY

unit orientation:
UPRIGHT

zone:
ENGAGED

Paul
Cezanne

1839 - 1906

Narrator Translation: Provence the son of a wealthy banker and tradesman. In 1861, after

Product: Autumn Chair
Designer: Allan Harp
School: Georgia Tech,
Georgia Tech Advanced
Wood Product Laboratory
Year: 2002

Who was your mentor?

Joseph Koncelik had a great effect on me as an educator—for
staying dedicated to education and for helping to shape the
profession. Joe taught the three *R*s: respect for people, rigor in
your work, and research of your design problem and solution. He
had integrity in his work that I don't often see in the field.

   Another mentor, Kimberly Elam, is a master studio instructor.
The most important thing she did was bring the best out of each
student. She let students know exactly what was expected of
them through a contract they read at the beginning of each class.
It really raised the bar for studio behavior.

What qualifications do you look for when accepting design students to your program?

I like students who care about others, can present ideas well verbally, and have good social skills, passion, and personal integrity. They need to be team players but also capable of their own self-expression and aesthetic vision.

What skills do you think are important for students to learn?

Students need a range of traditional skills and some new skills required for entry-level positions. Students still must be able to draw well enough to communicate their ideas and capture interest. They must be able to think and work in two dimensions and in three dimensions, both on paper and on the computer. Students who know their design history and have software, modeling, graphics skills, and design research skills will be highly employable if their portfolios also show they are good problem solvers and have a good aesthetic sense.

Product: Autumn Chair
Designer: Allan Harp
School: Georgia Tech, Georgia Tech Advanced Wood Product Laboratory
Year: 2002

School: Milwaukee Institute of Art and Design

EDUCATOR: PASCAL MALASSIGNÉ

Title: Professor
Program Name: Industrial Design
Location: Milwaukee, Wisconsin

Product: Box
Designer: Chris Heckman
School: Milwaukee Institute of Art and Design
Year: 2000
Description: Box combining all the elements of a video game storage system into one unit. Awarded second prize in the 2001 IHA student design competition.

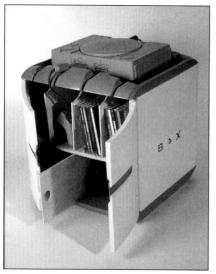

When did you discover design? When did you know it was what you wanted to do?

As a teenager in France, I was attracted by the form of automobiles and was fascinated by the more exuberant design of the few American cars in our towns as compared to European cars. I also noticed that the form of cars changed every so often, and it was fun to compare the forms of new models versus old and discuss the changes with friends. Then, through friends, I heard of artists called *designers* who were designing products, and I was sold.

Why did you become a teacher?

Charismatic people who articulate and communicate well have always fascinated me. Then, as a graduate student, I had an opportunity to teach, and I realized I was not doing a bad job at communicating and working with students. That has been going on now for over twenty-five years.

How do you teach design?

I concentrate on the project at hand and explain in detail the methodology or the approach that the students must follow to succeed. A good design education story: The Milwaukee Institute of Art and Design (MIAD) and the Adaptive Art Department of Milwaukee Public Schools collaborate on a project that helps our industrial design (ID) students realize that their future clients will include the entire population—young and old, able-bodied and

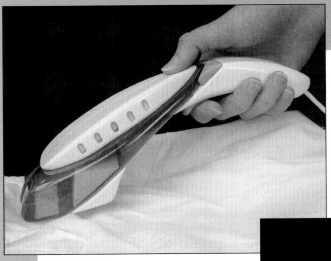

Product: Impulse Spot Remover
Designer: Lisa Heim
School: Milwaukee Institute of Art and Design
Year: 2001
Description: Deep-cleaning spot remover for clothing. Awarded second prize in the 2002 IHA student design competition.

Product: Cubby Laundry Hamper
Designer: Jason Crew, IDSA member
School: Milwaukee Institute of Art and Design
Year: 2001
Description: Portable, soft-sided, expandable laundry hamper that can accommodate large or small quantities of laundry. Received honorable mention in the 2002 IHA student design competition.

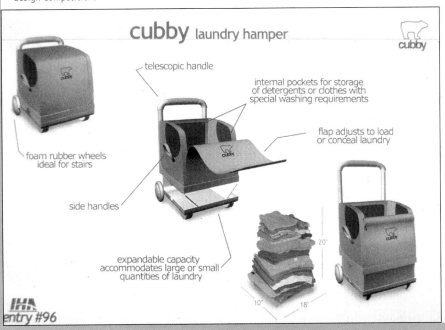

cubby laundry hamper

cubby

telescopic handle

internal pockets for storage of detergents or clothes with special washing requirements

flap adjusts to load or conceal laundry

foam rubber wheels ideal for stairs

side handles

expandable capacity accommodates large or small quantities of laundry

20"

10"   18"

IHA
entry #96

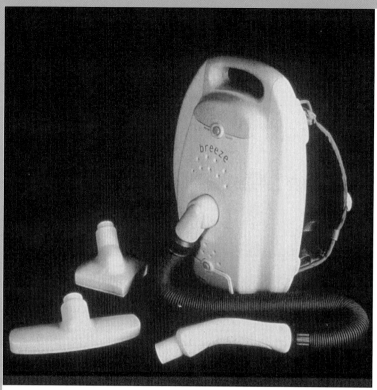

Product: Breeze Vacuum
Designers: Kari Thornborough,
Mike Phillips, Hector Rodriguez
School: Milwaukee Institute of
Art and Design
Year: 2000
Description: Cordless, bagless
backpack vacuuming system
that frees the user's hands and
increases mobility, making it
ideal for both disabled and
able individuals. Received
2001 ID magazine design
distinction award and
honorable mention in the IHA
student design competition.

disabled. They are asked to create assistive devices that help high school students with disabilities do art class assignments. They follow a process of design, prototype fabrication, and hands-on evaluation in the schools as part of developing the new devices. It gives the ID students great satisfaction to see their products being used and to know they are making a difference in the lives of students who have disabilities.

Who was your mentor?
Art Pulos, FIDSA.

What qualifications do you look for when accepting design students to your program?
Talent, creativity, imagination, and outstanding two-dimensional or three-dimensional skills.

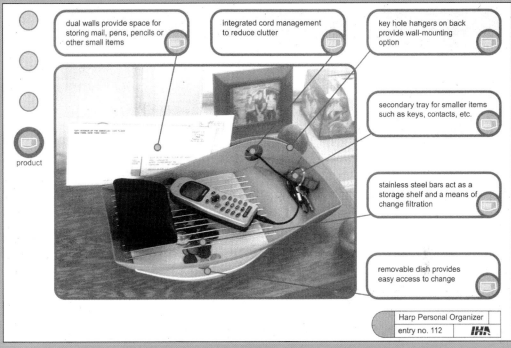

dual walls provide space for storing mail, pens, pencils or other small items

integrated cord management to reduce clutter

key hole hangers on back provide wall-mounting option

secondary tray for smaller items such as keys, contacts, etc.

stainless steel bars act as a storage shelf and a means of change filtration

removable dish provides easy access to change

product

Harp Personal Organizer
entry no. 112   IHA

What skills do you think are important for students to learn?
Problem solving, communicating effectively, being open-minded, understanding what client needs are and responding appropriately; traditional two-dimensional skills (sketching and rendering by hand) as well digital two- and three-dimensional skills (Illustrator, PhotoShop, Cobalt, Alias-Wavefront, etc.); traditional three-dimensional and model-making skills.

Product: Harp Personal Organizer
Designers: Mark Van Handel, Brian Ellis
School: Milwaukee Institute of Art and Design
Year: 2001
Description: Convenient storage system to corral personal items such as PDA, cell phone, credit cards, wallet, change, and keys. Received honorable mention in the 2002 IHA student design competition.

School: University of Bridgeport

EDUCATOR: JIM LESKO
Title: Head, Director, Art and Design
Program Name: Industrial and Interior Design
Location: Bridgeport, Connecticut

Product: Daisy Air Purifier
Designer: Manuel Saez
School: University of Bridgeport
Year: 2000
Description: A whimsical take on the air purifier, a traditionally boring product. Received first prize in the 2000 National Housewares Student Design Competition and the Idea 2000 Bronze Award.

Who is your design hero?
Donald Dohner, who started the design program at Carnegie Institute of Technology between 1932 and 1934 and at Pratt Institute in 1935. The curriculum he created is still in use in most design schools. His view of design was broad in that it included human factors, materials and processes, and marketing. He also recognized the importance of women in the marketplace. His design methods led to the savings of millions of dollars. He also was one of the first designers to recognize the importance of plastics in consumer products.

When did you discover design?
I remember seeing Mesa Verde in the encyclopedia. I couldn't read yet—I was too young—I just looked at the picture, which was frightening but compelling. I opened to that page over and over and wondered who did that to that mountain? The red color of the clay made it look hot and melted—but up, not down. I couldn't figure it out.

Later, when I moved to the city, I used to hang out in the kitchen housewares department at Kaufman's because I loved to hold the shiny, brightly colored cooking stuff. Stainless steel with fasteners right there, not hidden. Plastic woods and steel. Really neat stuff. The German stuff was real clean, and the Italian stuff was real sexy. But all the mass-produced stuff was all

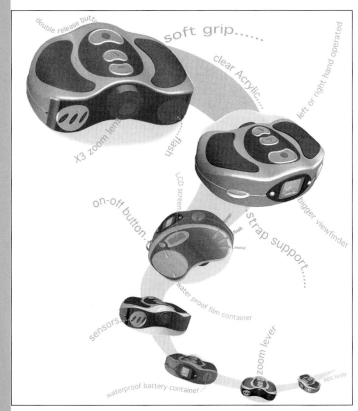

soft grip......

double release button

clear Acrylic......

left or right hand operated

X3 zoom lens

flash

bigger viewfinder

on-off button

LCD screen

strap support......

zoom lever

sensors

flash

rewind

water proof film container

waterproof battery container

ABS body

Product: CSL 35mm Camera
Designer: Manuel Saez
School: University of Bridgeport
Description: Camera uses a mirror to redirect light toward the film, which is located horizontally at bottom of camera. Received an award at the 2000 Prometheus Design Competition.

alike, no variation in size, maybe just different colors. I wanted to know more about the way it was made, but I thought somebody would think I was feminine because the stuff was for women and cooking. I didn't think of it that way, I just liked the way it looked and felt when I held it.

When did you know what you wanted to do?
I never wanted to do one thing; I wanted to do it all. I'm happy when I have a mission. I'd like to conduct a full symphony orchestra if I could read music.

Why did you become a teacher?
I think of myself as a student.

Product: Prickly Pals
Designer: Manuel Saez
School: University of Bridgeport
Year: 2000
Description: Desktop pencil holders made from aluminum extrusion and natural straw.

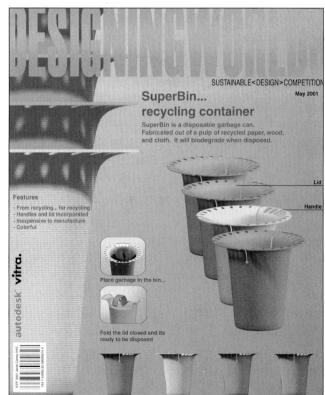

Product: SuperBin
Designer: Manuel Saez
School: University of Bridgeport
Year: 2001
Description: Garbage can made of paper pulp from recycled paper. Received an award at Designing Worlds Competition.

How do you teach design?
I'd rather be a guest critic than a studio teacher. I like defense, not offense. I like to figure out what someone is trying to do and really mess them up when they don't have a good answer. But when they do, I like to watch them cross the goal line.

What qualifications do you look for in a student?
I gave up trying to figure that out. I'm more interested in what I can learn from them.

What skills do you think are important for students to learn?
Excerpted from the department manifesto, written with Robert Brainard:

> *Our overarching goal in teaching industrial design is to provide each student with the intellectual preparation and skills required to enter the profession. While the computer has changed the requirements in the design field, traditional drawing and modeling skills are equally important and remain the focus in our educational philosophy.*

Product: Adonis
Designer: Manuel Saez
School: University of Bridgeport
Year: 2000
Description: A bicycle rack that also protects trees in New York City.

School: Philadelphia University

EDUCATOR: GOETZ UNGER

Title: Associate Professor and Director of
Industrial Design
Program Name: Industrial Design, School of
Architecture and Design
Location: Philadelphia, Pennsylvania

When did you discover design?
On registration day at the Gesamthochschule Kasselin Germany, a
beautiful, charming design junior explained that industrial design
was "inventing the mix of art and technology." That interested
me as much as she did.

Why did you become a teacher?
When I interested a company in developing a design of mine for
manufacture, I was offered the position of development manager.
As time passed, the distance between the creative design process
and myself grew. I knew from experience as an adjunct lecturer

Product: Collab Design Award
Designer: Kate Reynolds
School: Philadelphia University of Industrial
Design
Year: 2001
Description: Made of flexible laser-etched
high-temperature silicone and designed for the
annual COLLAB design competition, this object
symbolizes the continuity of design. This design
was awarded first place and will be given to all
future recipients of the award.

that I would enjoy teaching. That design educators are encouraged to pursue their own design work was the other, vital element in my decision.

How do you teach design?

It is a tricky task to prepare students for a profession that has become so diverse and to impart a forever widening skills and knowledge base in only four years. Teaching the process of learning and the process of design is the only strategy to prepare students for a lifetime in this profession.

While there is a generally accepted basic skill set and basic knowledge that all entry-level students should have, it is reasonable to devise a curriculum that empowers students—that allows them, especially as seniors, to explore design issues that resonate with their personal interests. Crucial to their explorations is a diverse faculty with good connections to industry. Also vitally important, especially for the last two years, is a dedicated studio space where students learn skills from one another; it encourages the design discourse needed to develop a design persona.

Eyes turn to us only when the physical and cultural relationship between the object, the environment, and the person is the issue. History and theory must be an integral part of the design studios early on so that subsequent exposure to engineering and business concerns can be understood as opportunities for better design.

Who do you think of when you are teaching?

Two heroes, Harry Bertoia and Dick Schultz, caused me to move from London to Pennsylvania twenty-two years ago. But heroes are perfect only in specific contexts; life is a mixed blessing. Disappointments, frustrations, and failures in life are as motivational as the successes—and certainly more numerous.

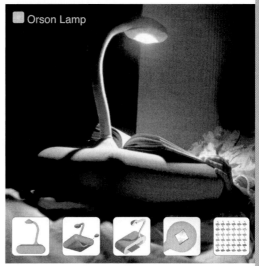

Orson Lamp

Product: Reading lamp
Designer: Emory Krall
School: Philadelphia University of Industrial Design
Year: 2001
Description: Fully positionable pillowlike lamp designed for reading in bed without disturbing a partner. Four white LEDs emit soft, cool directed light, powered by a flat rechargeable battery. Since LEDs release very little heat, fabric and foam could be used in construction.

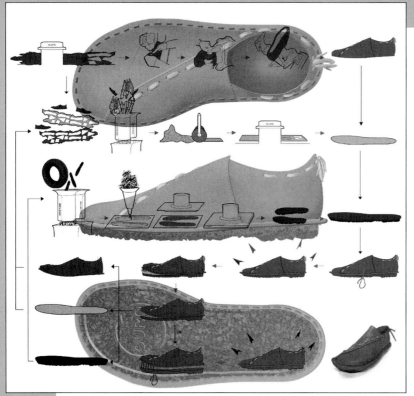

Product: Women's Footwear
Designer: Lea Bogdan
School: Philadelphia University of Industrial Design
Year: 2002
Description: Shoe made from scrap and reclaimed materials (crumb tire rubber, leathers) demonstrates sustainability, energy and material conservation, and cost efficiency

Product: Digital Infrared Thermometer
Designer: Michael Robinson
School: Philadelphia University of Industrial Design
Year: 2002
Description: Cast aluminum and Ultern (high-temperature, high-impact plastic) are utilized in the design of this thermometer, which addresses the issues of handling, interface, and connectivity between the user and technology.

What qualifications do you look for when accepting students to your program?
A good grade point average and an inquisitive, analytical mind are good predictors of doing well. The ability to draw and fabricate objects is a bonus, but I do not find these reliable indicators of talent. Most students can be taught a level of competence in these skills.

What skills do you think are important for students to learn?
Within IDSA's (Industrial Designers Society of America) guidelines, two categories contain descriptions of what I would call skills; these are acquired or improved with training:

- Methods and Processes
  – Problem definition
  – Conceptualization and evaluation
  – Testing and refining of solutions

- Communication
  – Two- and three-dimensional presentation of ideas
  – Oral communication
  – Written communication
  – Application of computers

Skills are a prerequisite to securing a job and being of service. Understanding the valuable role design can play in society is a prerequisite to becoming a design leader.

School: North Carolina State University

EDUCATOR: HAIG KHACHATOORIAN

Title: Professor and Chair
Program Name: Department of Industrial Design
Location: Raleigh, North Carolina

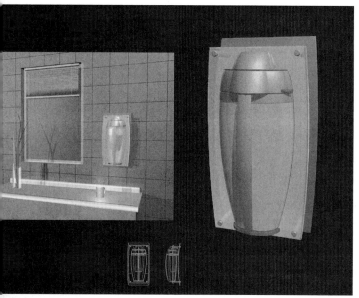

Product: Art of Making Coffee
Designer: Claudia Rebola
School: North Carolina State University
Year: 2000
Description: This coffee maker blends the emotional experience of enjoying coffee with technological performance and aesthetic value.

When did you discover design?
During my freshman year at Cass Technical High School in Detroit, Michigan, an instructor introduced me to the field of industrial design. It was a three-year program, with nineteen curricula, plus college prep for each specialization. The art department had three areas: design, fashion, and arts and crafts. At the end of the program, my particular graduating class took 11 percent of the art scholarships in the United States. I received a full scholarship to Pratt Institute. Harry Bertoia was a graduate, as was Lily Tomlin.

Why did you become a teacher?
I have always balanced a design career with an academic one. When practicing full time, I taught part time. I started my teaching career in San Francisco on returning from a Fulbright at the Academy of Fine Arts in Krakow, Poland. Teaching allows me to explore the realm of the mind. I believe the profession of design is equal to business, medicine, law, and engineering in terms of its contributions to society and civilization. Teaching allows me the opportunity to produce a model of professional behavior that is based on design excellence, accountability, social responsibility, and the humanization of technology.

How do you teach?

For the last five years, we have been conducting an advanced and integrated product design and development course. It is based on a cross-functional team process with faculty and students from the colleges of design management and engineering. The students work in multidisciplinary groups on corporate-sponsored projects. The course has been enormously successful in terms of clients and student design results.

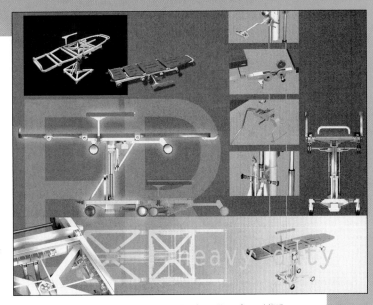

Who do you think of when you are teaching?

I approach design from a multidisciplinary and multilayered process, including both formal and informal techniques. Using the iterative process as a basic structure, I have added techniques from psychology and management sciences to enhance the impact of the content. I set the stage for my projects in terms of problem detection, definition, development, and dynamics (effects). My definition of design is the organization of life on a high level, as well as the things that support and enhance life.

Product: Transformable Emergency Stretcher
Designer: Claudia Rebola
School: North Carolina State University
Year: 2000
Description: Through careful use of ergonomics and the functional mechanisms needed in transport systems, this emergency cart serves the needs both of the ER and of the patient.

What qualifications do you look for when accepting design students to your program?

The department seeks students who enjoy and are curious about cultural artifacts, objects and products, mechanisms, materials and processes, inventions and innovations, technology, and marketing. Potential designers are interested in changing their world. They see technology as a way of improving life on many levels. They are motivated to create objects and products that solve human needs and address human wants. We look for students with diverse backgrounds and high academic achievement. Their portfolio gives us a talent indicator and intellectual guide to see how the student sees, thinks, creates, and communicates his or her ideas.

GIMA IS A SMART STORAGE SYSTEM, WHICH HOLDS
AN INDIVIDUAL'S MEDICAL INFORMATION RECORD
IN ORDER TO ASSIST NOT ONLY PATIENTS,
BUT ALSO DOCTORS IN TRACKING PURPOSES
FOR MEDICAL/PERSONAL ASSISTANCE.
IT IS UNIVERSAL PREVENTIVE SYSTEM
TO LINK THE ADVANCED EVOLUTION
OF THE MEDICAL ENVIRONMENT
WITH THE PATIENT ASSISTANCE.

GLOBAL INTELLIGENT MEDICAL AGENT

GIMA

Product: Global Intelligent Medical Agent
Designer: Claudia Rebola
School: North Carolina State University
Year: 2000
Description: GIMA is a smart storage system that holds an individual's medical information, is easily updatable, and is accessible by both patients and doctors.

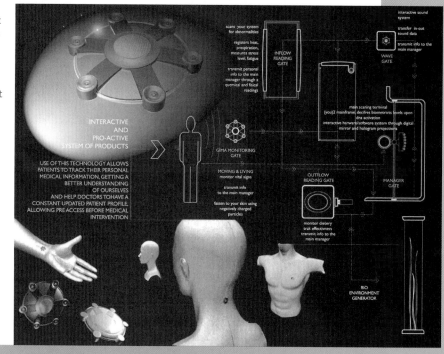

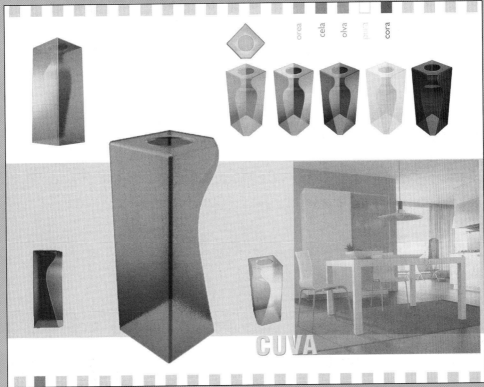

What skills do you think are important for students to learn?

- Analytical skills
- Conceptualization skills
- Drawing and delineation skills
- Organizational skills
- Communication skills (writing and speaking)
- Aesthetic sensibilities
- Leadership skills
- Mechanical aptitudes
- Social skills
- Environmental awareness
- Strategic-tactical thinking skills
- Model-making skills
- Computer skills

Product: CUVA 2000
Designer: Claudia Rebola
School: North Carolina State University
Year: 2000
Description: CUVA is a subtle ironic gesture in tribute to an object's history through a perceptual update with an acknowledgment to nostalgia.

Chapter Two

Lighting

How many times have you heard the phrase "Show time!"? It literally means "Light up the theater! We're ready for the show to go on!" When the stage lights come up, the audience is ready for exciting things to happen. Light is magical; lighting is everywhere, and without it we really can't see much.

Lighting design ranges from lighting homes to lighting corporate offices to lighting landscapes. Lighting designers work for large companies and also design independently. Sometimes, light fixtures are commissioned by architects and interior designers for specific spaces; restaurants and hotels are areas where designers might be asked to design specifically for the space. In those cases, the light fixture might eventually be manufactured for general sale.

Thomas Alva Edison had no idea what he started with the invention of the light bulb. Just think—before the light bulb we all depended on either gas lighting or candles, although light fixtures obviously played a significant role in the design of spaces even then. The electric light bulb allowed far more materials to be incorporated into the design of lighting without the fear of fire or other disaster. Now all light fixtures are approved by either UL (Underwriters Laboratories) or the CSA (Canadian Safety Association). The stringent regulations concerning the design and manufacturing of lighting must be adhered to at all times.

Light fascinates us as consumers and is equally fascinating to designers. The design of light fixtures ranges from the utilitarian to the fantastic. Walking into a building—whether a corporate headquarters, a museum, or a home—one of the first things we comment on is the lighting. It's too dark! It's bright! It's gloomy! These are all perfectly valid responses to the mood set by the lighting designer, intentionally or not. Light shapes our world; it gives it form, atmosphere, and context. Designing lighting is not just about the form the light fixture takes but also how it affects the mood of the space it occupies.

Historically, lighting design has always been about setting the tone of a space through the emanation of light and the form the light fixture takes. A glass chandelier creates an awesome presence, a certain kind of sparkling light reflected in the crystals. A globe of light creates a small sphere of luminescence that glows and floats, seemingly flooding the space. Wall sconces create small vignettes, depending on the style the designer intended to evoke. A simple lampshade sconce might evoke a certain era; gaslights or candles can create a wall pattern in a corridor. (Think of hotels, with their long repetitive corridors lit by wall sconces. The rhythm of the sconces leads you through the space.) Floor lamps are movable and allow people to create their own area of light for reading or tasks. Table or desks lamps are used for intimate lighting situations and again enable the interior designer or architect to create a certain type of effect.

Product designers don't often get to incorporate their light fixtures into spaces they've designed; other professionals usually specify the fixtures. Thus, designing light fixtures depends on many factors, including the market they will be used in, how they will be manufactured, where they will be manufactured (many lighting companies manufacture their products in Asia), and, of course, who will buy them. Traditionally, lighting fixtures were designed by the companies that produced them, but more and more companies are turning to freelance designers because they get to see many more ideas and just might stumble over a product the becomes a runaway best-seller.

The Tizio light by Richard Sapper for Artemide is this kind of success story. It became so popular that Artemide changed its logo to the Tizio shape. In 1971, the Tizio was one of the first light fixtures to use a halogen bulb. The halogen bulb ushered in a new way of looking at lighting design. It allowed designers to think small. From ceiling downlights to freestanding lamps, everything could be smaller in scale, and new design freedoms were unleashed.

The halogen revolution has matured; now liquid crystal displays (LCDs) are the future. Every manufacturer is always looking for that next great idea in lighting. LCD is a hot topic in the lighting industry because of its low power usage and the possibility of building into the light source the ability to change color at the whim of the consumer. Think how wonderful it would be to change the harsh white light being emitted from the task lamp into a soft, almost candle-like light without changing the bulb. Another area of research is *electroluminesence*, which conveys the ability to paint walls of light. This development opens new ways for designers to create amazing light fixtures.

Lighting designers look to certain people to see the future of lighting design. The architect Steven Holl uses light in spaces in creative ways, generating illusions that bring new understanding of the power of light. James Tyrell creates sculpture about light and how we see. Holl's and Tyrell's innovations inspire lighting designers; their thoughtful and fascinating uses of light provoke, startle, and question how we see—which, in the end, is what light is all about.

Designing Is Work

DESIGNER: ALECIA WESNER

Title: Director of Design
Firm Name: George Kovacs Lighting
Location: New York City

What is your favorite design?
My Space Boy lamp is the first I did for George Kovacs and the first I did without anyone's help. When I started here just out of school, they gave me direction about what they needed in the line. George was on a trip, and I had time to play around with different ideas. I came up with hanging styrene petals off the lamp. We found a bulb with a filter that created these incredible shades of light. George loved it, and we ended up winning an honorable mention from *Industrial Design* magazine. That's my baby!

Product: Space Boy
Designer: Alecia Wesner
Dimensions: 51" H, 8" dia. shade, 9" dia. base
Finish: Satin steel
Shade: 10 white translucent "petals"
Bulb: 50-watt MR-16 display lamp

What is your most successful product?
The biggest pendant we make—a 34-inch rim of metal with holes all over it called Holy—is our best-seller. We designed it because customers told us they needed a big chandelier. It's been specified in some really neat projects—a couple of nightclubs and a Lutheran Church in Ohio. I think it's funny that it's named Holy and it ended up in a church.

How do you design?
It's pretty random. When George and I were at a lighting show, we discussed what we really needed versus what I was working on. So I drew in the airport, the entire time on the plane, and on the way home. In forty-eight hours I showed George sketches, but he needed to see a mockup. He loves it. That's the new Joseph line.

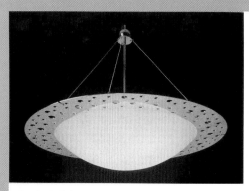

Product: Holy
Designer: Alecia Wesner
Dimensions: 29" h, 34" dia.
Shade: 5" dia. canopy, 10' cord
Finish: Polished brass or nickel
Bulbs: (4) 100-watt "A" bulbs

Do you find that reacting quickly to a new idea is important?
Absolutely! But I didn't always think that way. Now I react immediately. As soon as I can get the idea down is when it's really freshest. Even though I think I have it in my mind, a couple of hours later it's different.

Do you use the computer?
After sketching, I design using AutoCAD. My architecture training leads me to sketch on a grid because the little cubes measure something in my mind.

How did you decide to become a lighting designer?
I went to school for architecture and then switched to industrial design in my third year. I was very focused then, which really helped me excel. One class I wanted to take was lighting design. The class was filled, but I went anyway. It started at 8 A.M. and ended at 2 P.M. I watched as most of my classmates dropped out because those times. The projects I did for that class became a major part of my portfolio. Classes outside my major—lighting and sculpture—helped me get this job. At first I thought I didn't want to work for a manufacturer, but now I'm glad I do.

Product: Brave Reflections (286)
Designer: Alecia Wesner
Dimensions: 14" h, 5" dia.
Canopy: 10" dia. glass shade, 10' adjustable wire and cable
Finish: Satin steel
Glass: Gradient white or gradient yellow or opaque grey stripe with clear.

What's your design philosophy?
No matter how much natural talent you have, you have to pour a certain amount of work into design. But if you really love what you're doing, it never really seems like a job.

A huge part of my job is selling—not only selling what I make but also selling myself. At the shows, it's important to be able to talk about my work and to remember that most people don't understand technical drawings. You need people skills to be able to communicate and express your ideas. Communication is key. So much of design is asking questions, seeking sources, being curious. You need people skills to ask the right questions.

Where do you design?

My most creative time tends to be at home at night. I have room to spread out, sit on the floor or pull my coffee tables on wheels in closer, and sketch. I do all the CAD and technical things at work, but the creative things I do at home.

What inspires you?

Design comes from the strangest places. At a motorcycle show I noticed combinations of finishes because certain parts of bikes are very hot. What's beautiful is how the parts interact. I asked, "How does that translate to a lamp?" Lighting design involves similar issues—treating some materials differently because of heat properties. Besides going to shows, I get inspiration from architecture. A little thing like a door jamb might translate into a lamp.

When designing a light, do you think about where it might be used?

Definitely! Going to furniture shows helps because I see what is current and in the mainstream. What type of lamp are people who buy a crazy-looking red sofa going to place next to it? Do they want something that competes with it, or do they want something that is really going to celebrate it?

What was you best experience designing?

Brave Reflections was inspired by a poem about standing strong in a moment of self-reflection. The entire group is based on seeing the bare, clear, exposed bulb; you actually see the filament. I designed some simple shapes and took the drawings to Murano Glass in Venice, Italy. Though there was a bit of a language barrier, it was great to tell the artisan glassblowers that I wanted them to dictate the final shapes. I wanted each piece to be unique, with inconsistent stripes and colors. They couldn't believe I didn't want something very controlled. When I saw the final pieces with the different variations, I said, "Wow! I did that!"

What are you working on now?

I'm working on transitional lights named for my Uncle Joseph, a sculptor. What he does with huge pieces of metal is incredible. He's my hero. I wanted to go into an artistic field because of him. My style is different from his, but the raw finish of the pieces reminds me of his work—geometric, clean, all welded steel. We needed a group to go with a lot of furniture types, with both glass and paper shades, and the line had to meet a certain price point. There were a lot of parameters.

Product: Brave Reflections (300)
Designer: Alecia Wesner
Dimensions: 30" h, 9" dia. canopy, 18" dia. glass shade, 10' adjustable wire and cable
Finish: Satin steel
Glass: Clear top and opaque red bottom
Bulb: 60-watt clear "A" bulb

American Aesthetic

DESIGNER: HARRY ALLEN

Title: President
Firm Name: Harry Allen Design, Inc.
Location: New York City

Product: Dom Perignon Holiday Boxes
Designer: Harry Allen & Associates
Client: Shieffelin & Somerset Co.
Materials: Printed paper
Year: 1993
Photo: Carolyn Taylor for Bates 101

You design everything: interiors, furniture, products, packaging, graphics, restaurants, and boutiques. It's difficult to pigeonhole you. Is this intentional?
While I was completing my education, I was hired by Prescriptives to do their store design. So my training is one thing—I learned to design products in school—and my practical experience is something else. My career is split between two businesses: interiors and product design. Practically, it's a really good thing from a business point of view. I like the balance; one seems to feed the other. When I'm designing an interior space, I make choices about furnishings and accessories, and lots of times I see a need, so I design a piece of furniture or accessory for the space, and one thing leads to another. Yet I always consider myself a product designer first because of my training. That informs my other work. My work as an interior designer wouldn't be interesting if I weren't a product designer. The level of consideration is different. Everyone who works here is a product designer. When they come here, they've never worked on an interior project. We make it up as we go along.

Here's a good example of how the work grows and changes. I've been doing work for Dom Perignon Champagne for several years. First I did some windows; then I did some merchandising units, which totally fell within the parameter of industrial design. One day they called for an emergency meeting; they wanted us to design their Christmas packaging for 2002. I said yes.

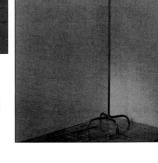

Product: Clear chandelier and color torchiere
Designer: Harry Allen, Harry Allen & Associates
Client: George Kovacs Lighting
Materials: Chromed steel, various glass pieces, and perforated metal
Year: 1998
Photos: Andrew Garn

Product: Hushhush store interior
Designer: Harry Allen, Harry Allen & Associates
Client: Kaz Design, Japan
Materials: Plywood, stainless steel, blackboard, acrylic, cement, mirror, vinyl flooring, and various lighting
Year: 2000
Photo: Nacasa and Partners

Product: Moss Interior
Designer: Harry Allen, Harry Allen and Associates
Client: MW Moss Ltd.
Materials: Painted sheetrock, powder-coated steel and glass
Year: 1999
Photos: Andrew Garn

Then we came back to the studio and we asked ourselves, "What are we going to do? We're not graphic designers." It turned out great. Dom Perignon sales were up 16 percent in December. I don't know whether it's based on this new design, but it made me feel really good. All of a sudden I'm a graphic designer. I love the idea of doing the next different thing.

You don't seem to have a style. Is this also intentional?
You should let the style develop from the project. Design is inspired by art. I love the thin line between art and design. Also, I never say no. I just say, "We can do that."

Presentation

DESIGNER: ANDREW SCHLOSS

Title: President
Firm Name: ABS Design
Location: New York City

What makes you happy that you chose to become a product designer?
I love the people part of design—meeting the factory workers and
the chief executive officers (CEOs). I love dressing differently
every day. One day I'm in a suit making a presentation; the next
day I'm in the factory working out design problems with the
engineers; the next day I'm making a presentation to sales and
marketing people. It is so much fun. Creating the presentations
for each group is like teaching a class in design. I try to explain
where the design comes from, what the historical references are.
With every project I learn something new.

What are you working on now?
Lighting and retail stores, and I am
passionate about both. Light is like
magic. No matter how much we all see
it—all day, every day—every time we
turn on a light we are surprised and
though we don't admit it, we say "wow"
ever so quietly.

I like to play with the light itself. I
believe light fixtures should be
absolutely functional and never
sculptures with light; however, they can
be sculptural, and they can manipulate
the light to create effects—glowing,
glaring, reflecting, shadows.

All of my best fixtures are low-tech.
They are all about some type of light
source and what happens to the light
that is emitted. It is a lot of fun. I am
always working on light fixtures.

Product: Pyramid Sconce
Designer: Andrew Schloss
Year: 2003

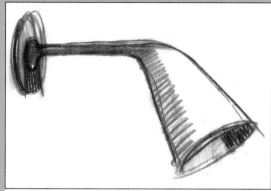

Product: Shower Head Sconce Sketch
Designer: Andrew Schloss
Year: 2003

Product: Shower Head Sconce
Designer: Andrew Schloss
Year: 2003

Describe your work with retail stores.

Much of my other work is retail spaces. I am interested in how design can directly influence shopping behavior, human experience, and corporate identity. The feel and experience of an environment (or product, for that matter) not only represents, builds, and supports a corporate identity but also can directly affect the experience of shoppers or users, increasing their likelihood to buy (increasing their level of satisfaction). All of this can, and usually does, take place on a subliminal level. I enjoy the retail work because it involves so much—aesthetics, psychology, branding/identity, advertising, economics, sociology, politics, and pure commerce.

How did your Zoompf ball project start?
The project started years ago. It started as a completely open-ended project that I assigned to myself. I wanted to design a new toy ball. I tried hundreds of shapes, cutouts, and materials, and in the end the origami idea came because I was fascinated with the idea of making a spherical object out of flat planes. You could approach a sphere in a geodesic kind of way or by cutting planes in the progressive sections of a sphere and then assembling them using spacers and other elements to create visual and tactile interest.

I designed about thirty variations. The company that manufactures the balls continued the ideas in-house and developed variations based on my schemes and progressions. Two of my original variations have design patents, and six models are currently being made by Hands On Toys.

Product: Zoompf Balls
Designer: Andrew Schloss
Year: 2003

Product: ABC Roller Bin Storage
Designers: Andrew Schloss, Jose Alcala, Sofia Dumert, Sun Chul Kim, Kimberly Leonard
Client: ABC School Supply, Inc., Duluth, GA
Year: 1998

Product: Grasshopper Chair
Designer: Andrew Schloss
Client: ABC School Supply, Inc., Duluth, GA
Year: 2001

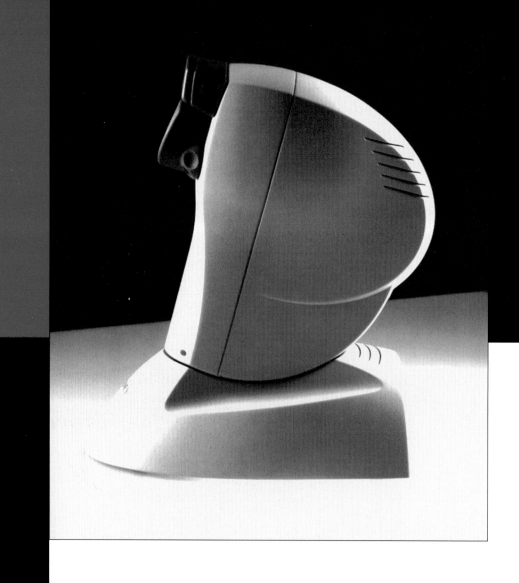

Chapter Three

Medical

Jeff Kapec says he's seen just about every surgical procedure that exists. Witnessing operations up close takes a strong stomach and a curiosity that most designers just don't have. Designing medical equipment encompasses all of medical and diagnostic medicine, from magnetic resonance imaging (MRI) to syringes. This is an area where you would think design is unnecessary but, as it turns out, it is desperately needed. Surgeons, medical technicians, and nurses in every area of medicine develop new and innovative methods of diagnosing and treating medical disorders every day, but they can't implement many of these innovations without the help of product designers. Product designers play a significant role in helping people get well and stay well.

Only a few centuries ago, barbers were also surgeons; probably the local blacksmith made their tools. As surgery and the practice of medicine became more controlled and more complicated and as people gained insight into how the human body functions, design became more important. The deliberate design of medical equipment probably emerged during the industrial revolution of the nineteenth century. As manufacturers became aware of develop-

ments in medicine, they responded with better and more cost-effective equipment.

Designers venturing into the operating room is a more recent development, probably spurred by their need to understand how the instruments and equipment are used. Observing and

Product: Discovery Speed-Vac Concentrator
Designers: Kazuna Tanaka, Jeffrey Kapec, Yukiko Naoi, Yoshi Matsuda
Project Engineer: Michael Glater, ThermoSavant
Client: ThermoSavant
Year: 1996
Photo: Reflex Photo, Bohemia, NY

discovering how doctors and nurses actually perform under the stress of surgical and medical procedures is the most beneficial aspect of visiting a medical facility. People who perform procedures are often unable to explain what actually goes on, so the trained designer's senses can make all the difference in a successful design.

As competition for the attention of medical personnel becomes more intense, design is playing an increasing role not only in how the tools are used but also what they look like. Color, texture, and material choice are playing a bigger role in what medical personnel purchase. Yes, styling of medical instruments and equipment is important. Decisions are made not only on how the tools perform but what they look like.

Leonardo da Vinci's anatomical drawings are still used today as prime examples of medical illustration. His investigations not only equipped him to produce more anatomically correct paintings but also led his inquiring mind to develop interesting designs based on human anatomy. Many designers cite Leonardo's work as having influenced their decision to become product designers. Interest in medicine, equipment, and the ability to visualize ideas seems to lead up the path to product design in the medical field.

Designing Is a Dialog

DESIGNERS: JEFF KAPEC
KAZUNA TANAKA
YUKIKO NAOI

Title: Partners
Firm Name: Tanaka Kapec Design Group, Inc.
Location: Norwalk, Connecticut

How do you approach design?
To the Tanaka Kapec Group, design is simplicity, simple surprises, and designing simply. Kazuna Tanaka believes our approach to design is simplicity, Jeff Kapec thinks we look for simple surprises, and Yukiko Naoi says it's designing simply. Our studio, a converted truck garage, appears to be anything but simple. Most of our clients manufacture medical devices designed to save lives.

Product: Rudolph Technologies, Inc. (Thin Film Metrology Instrument)
Designers: Jeffrey Kapec, Kazuna Tanaka, Yukiko Naoi
Year: 1996
Photo: Kenro Izu

How do you design medical devices?
We go into surgery and observe the operations. We try to understand what the surgery feels like to the doctors, nurses, and patients. Most of the time we don't know what nuances we are looking for until they evolve in our early discovery work. Playing, reenacting the physical activity, is the key to understanding what happens in the surgical clinical field.

How did you start designing medical products?
We worked on medical products at Human Factors, a product design firm in New York City. We have observed just about every surgery and acquired insight into how surgical procedures are handled and what goes on in operating rooms. Based on our expertise, some clients came to us when we set up the firm twenty-two years ago.

What is it like in surgery?

We try to think like the surgeons to understand their feelings and sensibilities. We then try to recreate in the studio the techniques we observed in the operating room to try to feel what they feel. That's the only way to design medical devices because they are really tactilely oriented.

It's important to be in the operating room because we see things that cue us to critical areas we would not see any other way. We are trained to keep our senses open to look for cues, and time and time again we have made discoveries the manufacturers weren't aware of.

An example is the biopsy forceps for C. R. Bard. The manufacturer wanted us create a better-looking device that was more comfortable for the doctor and less expensive to manufacture. We developed about twenty study models and then observed the surgery. The doctor steers the tip of the scope to the specific site to be biopsied and tells the nurse to pull. We discovered we had not only to satisfy the doctor's demands for appearance but also to address the nurse's anatomy. The manufacturer never realized this subtle distinction.

The Symphony Graft Delivery System is a new product for reconstructive spinal surgery. This device is designed to deliver an osteoconductive or osteoinductive growth factor, a mixture of blood and bone, as an implantable graft log. To design it, we had to observe extensive spinal surgery and lower spine and fusion surgery.

Product: Precisor biopsy forceps
Designers: Kazuna Tanaka, Jeffrey Kapec, Sam Montague
Client: C. R. Bard
Year: 1994
Photo: Kenro Izu

How do you get involved in manufacturing devices?

It's unusual for a design firm to actually manufacture devices. Doctors sometimes look for a

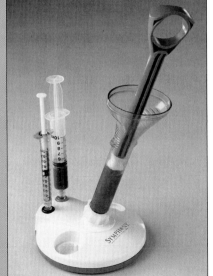

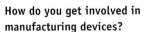

Product: Symphony Graft Delivery System
Designers: Kazuna Tanaka, Jeffrey Kapec, Yukiko Naoi, Yoshi Matsuda, Adam Stephens, John Voellmicke,
Engineer: DePuy AkroMed
Client: DePuy AkroMed
Year: 2001
Photo: Ron Hagerman, Providence, Rhode Island

design firm to help them package the technology so they can use it to conduct a study. We made fifty prototypes of an experimental device to relieve pressure in the ear that were used in a controlled study that was then submitted to the National Institutes of Health (NIH).

How do you manage the complex process of designing and manufacturing?

We carry on a dialog in the studio. No project simply goes through one person solely. It's the combined talent of a bunch of people, each with a slightly different viewpoint, slightly different strengths, always bumping into each other and affecting each other. We designed the space so this would occur.

Talk about creativity a bit.

We have an obligation as designers to make things look beautiful and be functional. How to combine the two is the dialog we have. In the manufacturing area, everyone likes to do what he or she has done before. It's the industrial designer's job to come up with something new and push the manufacturers to advance their process.

How do beauty and style enter the picture?

Everyone responds to attractive design. The subtle feedback from the form allows the surgeon control and sensitivity. So the instrument not only has to be beautiful but has to give that subtle feedback through the handle. Early on we investigated power tools, but the surgeons rejected the idea because there was no feedback, no feel.

Is it new for surgical tools to be so highly styled?

This is a competitive market, so you have to sell something that complements the functions and stimulates the senses and the intelligence. Surgical tools are a consumer product in many ways.

You also design consumer products. Is the process much different?

The process is similar. Instead of going into the operating room, we try to watch people. We make a lot of field trips. The process is basically the same: make models, test them, and show them to the consumer. The Franzus travel steamer was an interesting product because we decreased the size by 50 percent. The biggest hurdle was proving to manufacturing that it could be done.

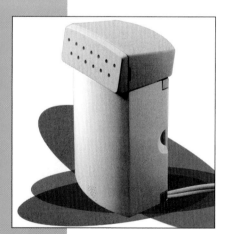

Product: Travel steamer
Designers: Jeffrey Kapec, Kazuna Tanaka, Yukiko Naoi, Pazit Kagel
Client: Franzus Company, Inc.
Year: 1996
Photo: Yukiko Naoi

What is your favorite project?

The TriMedic Triangle is still in the early testing stages. It's an adjustable support triangle used in surgery to prop the leg or arm so the surgeon can gain access to it. This device replaces expensive, elaborate rails. We designed it to be produced with radiotransparent plastic so doctors can shoot an X-ray and see exactly where they are in the operation. All the systems this replaces block the doctor's view. Doctors are going crazy over this product. They see it as a sophisticated plaything.

What motivates you?

Bridging the gap between design and reality. We understand both worlds, and we always want to bridge them. Otherwise we'd have little reason to get up in the morning.

What do you do every day that makes you happy that you chose to be a product designer?

We learn something new every day. We like that we design for real people and solve problems that affect people every day.

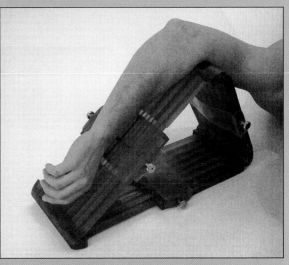

Product: Adjustable orthopedic support triangle
Designers: Kazuna Tanaka, Jeffrey Kapec, Yukiko Naoi, Adam Stephens, Brad Bender, TriMedics
Client: TriMedics
Year: 2000
Photo: Yukiko Naoi

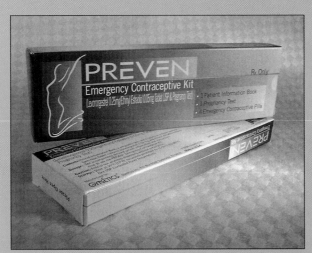

Product: Preven contraceptive kit packaging
Designers: Yukiko Naoi, Jeffrey Kapec
Client: Gynetics, Inc.
Year: 1998
Photo: Yukiko Naoi

Appropriateness

DESIGNER: MARIO TURCHI

Title: Principal
Firm Name: ION Design
Location: Edgewater, New Jersey

How do you work?

Whenever I get a new project, I like to let it sit for a while, about a week or so, to let it get ripe, like a piece of fruit. During that time, whether I am driving, shopping, or working on other projects, I like to think about it, look for other references or similar products, and start forming my own point of view. This is an important part of the project even though no time actually shows up on my time sheet. Once I'm ready (and hopefully not getting stale), I sit down with pencil and paper and start sketching and jotting down my thoughts. At that point we have an official project briefing with the entire design team, which may consist of other designers and mechanical engineers, depending on the size of the project. Each designer then goes off to work on his or her own, and we reconvene after a few days to compare notes and present our ideas to the entire team. This usually results in a brainstorm session that triggers many new ideas. After input and suggestions from the entire team, designers then integrate some of the group thinking in their design—and a design concept is born.

Product: N-Vision UB 30 Binoculars
Designers: Mario Turchi, Dennis Naksen, Robert Pandorf
Client: N-Vision
Year: 1999

Designing consumer products must be a challenge, given the high volume and design constraints.
One of the challenges you face is that if you do not like what you came up with—or worse, there is a mistake—it gets multiplied hundreds of thousands of times. There are always constraints; that's what design is all about.

ION Design doesn't seem to specialize. Is this a choice?
I think it's easier to survive as a design consultant if you don't specialize. Though it requires extra effort to stay current in the various industries you work in, every project benefits from the cross-pollination of ideas and a greater ability to think outside the box that comes from working for a variety of industries.

You have designed medical products. How do you go about designing something that seems to be about function only? Or is it?
Just like early consumer products that seemed to be more about function and then became more sophisticated over time, medical products have experienced a similar evolution. The refined look and feel of consumer products has raised user expectations in all product categories. In addition, product specifications for medical devices often have requirements like "appearance to be friendly and nonthreatening to the patient" written into the spec. Visual appeal is often part of the function.

When you are designing, who finally says "this is it"?
The budget! We are mostly a fee-for-service design firm, and clients expect us to stick to our budget. If it weren't for the budget or a deadline, a design project would never really be done.

Do you have a favorite client or design experience? Something that had a surprise at the end?
A company once came to us wanting a full-functioning prototype of a new type of endoscopy simulator for a trade show in two month's time. There was no other product like it on the market, so we were in uncharted territory. The design had to come together in two weeks, engineering was compressed to three weeks, and the prototype was completed in three weeks, just in

Product: Advisor 150; Saab Head-Mounted Display
Designers: Mario Turchi, Paul Katz, Dennis Naksen, Robert Pandorf
Client: Saab Avionics
Year: 2003

time for the show. Even though I thought the design was a bit slapped together and I was determined never again to get involved with a project that had such a crazy deadline, the product ended up winning a gold IDEA award from *BusinessWeek* and IDSA, much to my surprise.

Do you do a lot of research?

We usually do design research to see what's already out there. Launching a new product requires a substantial capital investment that most companies are not willing to underwrite unless they have some assurance through focus groups that their product will succeed.

What's in the future for industrial design?

As manufacturing processes become more sophisticated and traditional marketing strategies more complex, product designers will need to work more holistically, more closely within a multidisciplinary team made up of specialists in CAD and other software, mechanical and manufacturing engineering, and marketing. The designer will have to work closely with the various disciplines to develop the best possible product.

Who are your clients? What's different about your designs?

Most of the projects our firm gets involved with have to do with

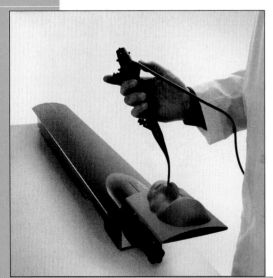

Product: PreOp Endoscopy Simulator
Designers: Mario Turchi, Diego Fontayn, Steven Bellofatto
Client: Immersion Medical
Year: 2000

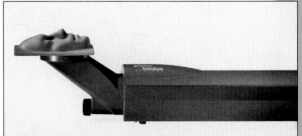

packaging the technology to make it more user-friendly. Our clients include manufacturers of medical and diagnostic instruments, sound systems, VR headsets, infrared vision systems, telephony products. But we have also designed travel mugs and dishwashing detergent bottles. Our designs tend to have a sculptural, elegant quality that makes them look expressive. Though we like to push the design envelope a bit, we are always careful not to push past it. I think the design of the products we work on is usually appropriate for their intended use.

What do you do every day that makes you happy you chose to be a product designer?
Designing a product is like solving a riddle. Every day brings a new challenge.

What is your most successful design? Why?
The design I'm most proud of is a single-dose insulin injector that was ergonomically considered, cleverly engineered, looked and worked great, and, most importantly, was specifically designed to help people in third-world countries cope with a debilitating disease.

Where do you get your ideas?
I get many ideas from carefully observing the world. Ideas are a bit like radio waves; they're all around us. The more I'm able to contemplate and focus on a given problem, the clearer the solution becomes.

Can you sum up your design philosophy in one word?
Appropriateness. It takes considerable skill to design a product in a way that is appropriate for its intended use. Whether a futuristic concept car or a surgical instrument, every design assignment requires a unique approach, and every designer must recognize when to pour it on and when to use restraint. After all, there is such a thing as too much design.

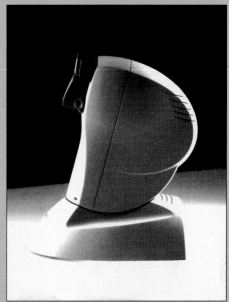

Product: Tomey Corneal Examiner AutoTopographer
Designer: Mario Turchi, Paul Katz, Dennis Naksen, Robert Pandorf
Client: Tomey
Year: 1998

It's Not the Thing,
It's the Who

DESIGNER: BILL CLEM
Title: Design Director
Firm Name: Strategix I.D., Inc.
Location: Bozeman, Montana

How did you discover industrial design?
It discovered me. During junior high I used a snowmobile to deliver morning papers throughout our rural Montana neighborhood, but it was noisy, stinky, heavy, and hard to drive. I developed a passion for improving it; I knew it could be better. I started sending my sketches to Polaris. Polite responses were sent back along with press kits, T-shirts, and even a racing jacket. Then I sent models, mechanism designs, and even advertising campaign ideas. The encouragement of Mike Vaughn and Bob Eastman led me to believe I could become a real designer, and Bob hired me for three summer internships from freshman to senior year and ultimately gave my first job as an industrial designer. I've been lucky to have such great people both as mentors and coworkers.

How do you work?
Discover, create, and deliver. First, we try to understand what the big question is—not the client brief or the stated objective but the underlying reason the project was conceived. Only then can we fully begin to research what the real issues are, why the objective is important, and who the real customers are. Our team members consider themselves customer advocates. Only by truly understanding customers can we understand the emotional and other needs of the audience. With design so directly affecting people in emotional ways, it's important to understand what drives those emotions and how we can respond to them effectively.

Our entire team gets involved and stays with the project until it's done. This simple but oft-ignored principle allows the application of each discipline to build a total project. Many times the research team hands off the information to the design team, which hands it off to the engineering team. There is only one team here.

What do you design?
I firmly believe it's not the thing you design but rather the who you design for. It's the idea that we're going to learn something new about people and apply it in a way specific to a certain

Product: AirGua Home Water Generator
Designers: Kent Swenseid, IDSA, Aki Hirota
Creative Director: Bill Clem, IDSA
Client: Airgua Inc.
Photo: Kent Swenseid
Year: 2002

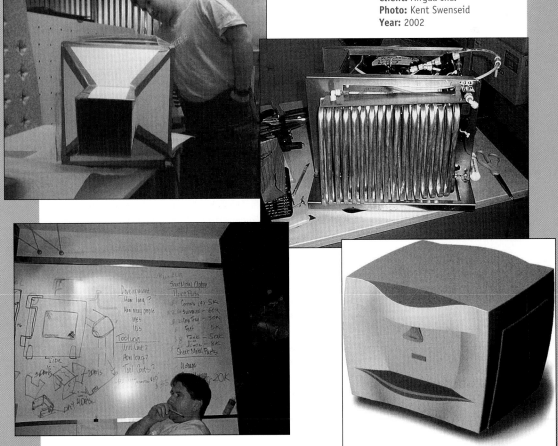

context. We don't specialize in any particular area for three good reasons. First, it would be unfair to tell our clients that we put our heart and soul into their products, only to turn around and do it again for somebody else in that same industry. Second, life would be pretty boring doing the same products over and over for competitors. Third, diversity in projects shows the similarity in people. Typically, a design firm that does a many types of things will tell you they can take processes or ideas from one area and apply it to another. While that's true, what we find is that we know people better because we experience them in all kinds of contexts, and that's worth a lot more to our clients and to their customers. The short answer is we design anything that fits our mission: helping people live life.

When you are designing, who finally says "this is it"?
Ultimately, it's the client's trust in us and our faith in doing what we believe is right that drives the final decision. Even so, it's a leap of faith. I don't believe in focus groups, trending data, or any sort of design-by-what's-being-done. Instead we focus on psychology, philosophy, anthropology, and other areas to find deeper meaning in what we are working on.

Do you do a lot of research?
Our research is tailored to find the constants by qualitative means, not quantitative methodologies. Even though there is a start and an end, new points are always being brought up throughout the process that must be integrated. We don't just do research and get on with it. There has to be some connection, and one part of the process should not stop while the other begins.

When you are designing, how do you do it?
First, we sit down to see if we understand what the client wants us to do. Silly as it sounds, that's the most difficult aspect of the project. What do they want us to do, and what do we think we should do? How far do they want us to take things, and how far do we really need to go to deliver something compelling? We usually determine that we want to do more—usually because we don't fully believe in the premise. That's not to say we don't believe our clients know what they want, it's just to say we don't think they always know what their customers want.

Next, we try to define the overall context of the total product. I can't explain exactly what we do, but context is everything, and there are hundreds for every product we've done. From the first time a customer hears about a product to the time they dispose of it, each context provides some further illumination as to a potential solution.

We'll develop metaphors and engage in storytelling sessions to flesh out the important ideas we want to communicate. Our brainstorming sessions are tailored to these storytelling sessions, providing a theater for discovery and also some humorous moments.

We don't have a set process for how we want to do something. Sometimes we'll do a few whiteboard sketches and move into digital models. Sometimes we'll make a few foam models and then go into the digital models. It just depends on the situation. For big things we like to go digital as quickly as possible.

Chapter Four

Consumer Products: Everyday Design

Every day we wake up and go through our daily routine—washing, eating, playing, working, going to school—and usually it's pretty normal. We rarely think about the products we use after we purchase them. We might think about them as beautiful, efficient, useful, and economical, except that when they don't work, we can get upset at them. It's probably then that we blame the designer for screwing up. When the toaster doesn't work or burns our toast we cry out, "Who designed this thing?" Design is transparent most of the time. Designing products for the consumer market is challenging; creating a successful product that allows consumers to get on with their lives and not interfere with it, is the biggest challenge facing designers in the consumer product field.

Testing ideas for consumer products is the biggest part of designing them. Everyone has

Designer Mark Lim in his studio at Conair Corporation, Stamford, Connecticut.

an idea to make daily life easier, but whether or not it is designed and engineered well has as much to do with its success as the original idea.

Consumer product designers spend hours producing quick prototypes of ideas that are then tested by focus groups of intended users or in natural situations. If the design is a kitchen product, the product is tested immediately in a kitchen; likewise, a bathroom product is tested in the bathroom. Context, context, context. Product designers design in the context in which the product will be used. Endless sketching and quick prototypes are the daily routine.

Most consumer products start with a dumb idea or a perceived problem. Product designers often do research just by watching and observing how something is done. They might do a time and motion study of how someone goes about making a pie or a cake or a spaghetti dinner, recording the process on video and then playing it back for the cook and asking questions about the how, why, where, when, and who. These studies lead the designer to make sketches and suggestions about how to improve the process.

An idea might be a simple thing that improves the product 5 percent, but enough to warrant further investigation. If the consumers and the manufacturer believe the idea has merit, prototypes are made and tested. Lots of ideas end up on the cutting room floor, discarded altogether or incorporated into a more complex idea. Smart designs such as the simple addition of a weight to a rolling pin allowed the handles to be placed off center, keeping the user's knuckles from interfering with the rolling process. At first glance the revamped rolling pin looks much like any other rolling pin; when it is its used, however, the simple improvements become evident. The same is true of a new design for a measuring cup. Placing the measurements on a slanting plane inside the cup allows users to see the current measurement as they pour ingredients into the cup, thus eliminating the need to pick up the cup to see the measurement. This simple improvement did not seem obvious until the cup was used.

Refining a computer-generated model in the shop. (Courtesy George Schmidt Design, Douglaston, New York)

Once the prototype is approved by the manufacturer, more complete and sometimes preproduction prototypes are constructed and test-marketed. It's at this point that many other people get involved—marketers, salespeople, and more engineers—all playing a significant role in the success of the product. Packaging, displays, and merchandising are all part of selling what started out as a simple, dumb idea.

Product: Unilever True Reflections (Kiosk analyzes skin and recommends products.)
Designers: Mark Dziersk, Marianne Grisdale, Ann Marie Conrado
Company: Herbst LaZar Bell, Inc, Chicago
Alias rendering: Andrius Stankus

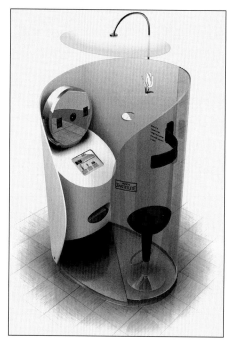

Materials is another area designers should be familiar with. Plastic in all its forms has had a profound effect on what consumer products look like. Forms that were impossible a few years ago are now easily and quickly manufactured. But plastic is just one material among the myriad used to manufacture consumer products; others are metal, paper, rubber, wood, glass, and porcelain.

In the end, product designers are form givers, and form is usually what first attracts a consumer. Color and texture are a few of the traits that affect that first impression. Product designers must be in tune with their own sense and be trained to be sympathetic to the unlimited ways in which consumers interact with the products they use. All the senses come in to play when a consumer uses a product. A simple change in texture on a handle can inform users and convey a message that is otherwise lost or impossible to convey another way. Consumer product designers have a responsibility to get us through our day as easily, safely, and with as little cost as possible by creating products that are easy to use, safe, and cost-effective. Consumers should to be able to choose from a wide variety of well-designed products that fit their budget with the assurance that all the products are safe and easy to use.

If consumer product design interests you, keep shopping and looking. Most consumer product designers spend a lot of time just wandering around stores and streets looking for ideas and cultural shifts. "What's next?" is one of the questions they ask themselves every day.

Consumer product design is a large field. As in others areas of design, designers can find employment in factories, small design offices, and large design offices. Large companies like Rubbermaid employ in-house product designers in specialized areas such as storage, kitchen, and bath.

Many product design companies provide all these services to clients. As design offices become bigger and more diversified, their staffs do as well. It is not uncommon for product design firms to employ psychologists, cultural anthropologists, engineers, marketing specialists, and even doctors. The environment at product design firms is rapidly changing from what used to be a group of designers and model makers to a complex group of intertwined professionals, all working to produce more sophisticated and efficient products.

Entering the consumer products field has become much more challenging because designers must be sympathetic to many more issues than they were just a few years ago. Teamwork is a must in the consumer product area because of the complexity of the projects and the speed at which products are produced. Being nimble and quick are two important attributes of the emerging product designer. Getting along in a team-oriented environment is essential. As in most areas of product design, a thorough understanding of computers and the part they play in mass production is absolutely necessary for designers entering this area. You don't have to understand the inner workings of computers and machinery of mass production, but you do have to understand their role and how they limit or enhance the final product.

Common Sense

DESIGNER: DAVIN STOWELL
Title: Chief Executive Officer
Firm Name: Smart Design LLC
Location: New York City

When did you know you wanted to be a product designer?
From the time I was teenager I knew I would become a product designer because I always wanted to make things. My sister worked at Corning Glass as a graphic designer, and she worked with industrial designers, so I knew what they did.

What is your favorite design?
A little pyrocream bowl I did for Corning called the Grab It. I designed it during Christmas vacation of my senior year at Syracuse University in 1975. (I worked summers at Corning with Herb Mann.) Most people heat their soup in a pan and then put it in a bowl. I thought, why not just heat it in a bowl you could eat from? (This was before microwaves.) It's not a new concept; it was based on little pewter ramekins that early Americans kept near the fireplace for keeping their soup warm. There was nothing in modern materials like that.

You know how you wake up in the middle of the night and you just know something? I imagined a bowl with a little handle, kind of pinched, like the petal of a flower. Market research tested the bowl, and people in the focus groups were just horrified and said they'd never use anything like that. But the head of the marketing group redesigned the focus groups, and people loved it. The factory claimed they couldn't possibly press the handle out of glass. Everyone hated it until they made the one I designed. It's the most successful piece in the history of the company. Designing it was just identifying a simple need and fitting a product to it. It's my favorite because it was the first real product I thought of and designed.

Product: Grab-It
Designer: Davin Stowell
Creative Director: Herb Dann
Client: Corning Glassworks
Year: 1975
Photo: Smart Design

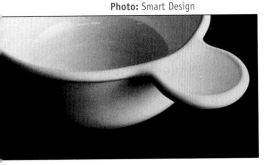

What would you like to design?

I can make anything that walks through the door better.

What are your most successful designs?

In terms of sheer quantity sold, the OXO peeler is probably one of the highest. The Johnson & Johnson toothbrush called Wondergrip has sold 10 million, which is the highest.

Where do you get your ideas?

Just look at the world; the ideas are right in front of you. Just watch people use things and then create things for their functional aspects. The aesthetic attributes are usually in nature.

How would you describe product design?

Making something a little better. Understanding and enhancing the emotional bond between product and user. People are intelligent; they know what they want.

How do you create products?

We work three-dimensionally to get a feel for the size and shape. Then we work two-dimensionally. The reason I make things first is that I found out early I couldn't draw, so I immediately learned how to make things out of clay and plaster. You learn quickly that the real thing just means so much more. We all doodle and sketch, but it never expresses what it feels like, what the proportions are like. If you look around here, we have all the tools, computers, and so on, but everyone carves stuff out of foam first to know if the proportions are right; then we go into CAD. We try to

Product: Reach Wondergrip
Designer: Smart Design
Client: Johnson & Johnson
Year: 1990

Product: OXO Good Grip Peeler
Designer: Smart Design
Client: OXO International
Year: 1991

Product: WOVO Bowls
Designer: Scott Henderson, Smart Design
Client: WOVO
Year: 2000

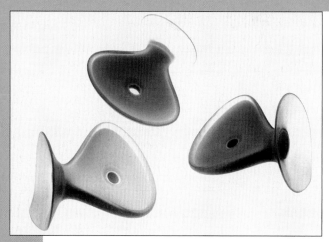

Product: OXO Good Grip bathroom accessories
Designer: Smart Design
Client: OXO International
Year: 2000

understand the goal. What are we trying to create? Then we can recognize the solution when we see it. If you don't understand the goal, you can't filter out the noise—all the solutions that are inappropriate. We try to make something a little better. We aren't looking for the next breakthrough. We're looking for the incremental step, the next logical product.

What's the best way to educate young designers?

I find young designers sometimes have trouble understanding the goal because they have their own agenda, which may have nothing to do with what the product is for, who it's going to be used by, or who is going to make it. To educate young designers, we often invite real people into the design process to talk about ideas. After young designers see real people mock their designs, they start to pay attention.

Why and how do you design things?

I always aspired to design something that would be sold at K-Mart rather than something that would be sold in a design store. I think there's a lot of satisfaction in getting that kind of acceptance. That's what our business is all about—pleasing enormous quantities of people. Our work is really research-intensive so we can understand our end users.

With respect to the OXO products, you commented, "The secret isn't the handle; it's really about producing a sharp blade; the handle is secondary." Did that come from research or intuition?

It's just common sense.

What was your last design purchase?

I don't buy designed things. I would rather buy an old cabinet that was made 200 years ago—just funky stuff somebody made for himself because that's the way he liked it. I think it's really hard for a trained designer to do something that real.

Product: Shampoo Bottles
Designer: Smart Design
Client: Johnson & Johnson

Product: HP Photosmart 100
Designer: Smart Design
Client: Hewlett Packard

Product: Timberland Performance Watches
Designer: Smart Design
Client: Callanen

Are you living your dream as a designer?
Yes. If there was any kind of dream, it was to do my own thing—start an office. It was a combination of being at the right place at the right time and taking advantage of the opportunities. You have to be opportunistic to succeed.

Can you sum up your design philosophy in one word?
Common sense. That's two words, but design is about looking for the commonsense solution to a problem.

Transforming

DESIGNER: MARK J. S. LIM

Title: Industrial Design Research and
Development Manager
Firm Name: Conair Corporation
Location: Stamford, Connecticut

How do you work? How do you attack a design problem?
1. I study and research the object I will design.
2. I draw form study sketches.
3. I draw dimensional sketches.
4. I create three-dimensional models; most of the time I use the Pro-Engineer program; then I use the SLA machine to build a prototype.

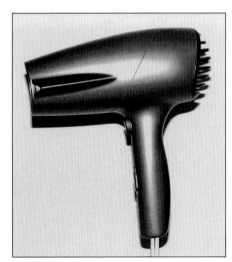

Product: Hair dryer prototype
Designer: Mark J. S. Lim
Company: Conair Corporation
Year: 2000

Each of the design projects always includes some of the problems I begin with. I solve the design problem by refining through this process.

I normally design products by myself because they are small items.

Designing consumer products must be a challenge, given the high volumes and design constraints.
I work very closely with Conair's New Product Marketing Group and focus groups before starting a project.

You design a wide range of products. How do you go about designing something that seems to be about function only? Or is it?
Most of our products are utilitarian items; therefore, the function of the product is very important. They should also be ergonomically sound.

Product: Trimmer (design model)
Designer: Mark J. S. Lim
Company: Conair Corporation
Year: 2000

When you are designing, how do you work? Do you mock things up in your shop?
I have a design studio and adjoining model shop. We also have a facility to make finished prototypes.

What's in your future? What do you want to design?
I would like to design something that would benefit the whole human society.

What's in the future for industrial design?
I think product design will be more important than engineering because the engineering of most products is already mostly done.

Who are your clients?
I am an employee of Conair, but it feels like I have many clients because Conair has so many divisions. A designer should increase the aesthetic value of products. When a man climbs the mountain, the higher he goes, the farther he can see.

How do you feel about seeing your work in use?
It's exciting. I feel responsible for better design.

What do you do every day that makes you happy you chose to be a product designer?
As an instrument, my mind, hands, and eyes are coordinated to bring a floating idea down to reality.

What inspired you to be a designer?
Art and science.

What is your most successful design?
It hasn't come out yet.

Where do you get your ideas?
From nature and the human body.

How do you work? In collaboration? Alone?
Alone and in collaboration. It depends on the project. If a project is big, we need collaboration.

Product: GNT 200 Trimmer
Designer: Mark J. S. Lim
Company: Conair Corporation
Year: 2000

Do you sketch?
I start with a sketch for all my projects. I
experience each line as if it feels like a door
opening to the creative world.

What are you working on now?
A hair dryer, a straightening iron, a trimmer, and a
shaver.

**Can you sum up your design philosophy in one
word?**
Transforming.

Product: Foot massager
Designer: Mark J. S. Lim
Company: Conair Corporation
Year: 2000

Product: Makeup mirror
Designer: Mark J. S. Lim
Company: Conair Corporation
Year: 2000

Beauty

DESIGNER: TUCKER VIEMEISTER

Title: President
Firm Name: Springtime-USA
Location: New York City

How did you discover industrial design?
My father, Read Viemeister, designed cars, machines, buildings, museum exhibits, packages, logos, and other printed stuff, and he invented things and did city planning. Even as a baby I could see he was doing the most interesting and fun stuff.

How do you work?
I am realizing there are many valid approaches to design. For instance:
1. Analyze some problem or lifestyle.
2. Look for ergonomic improvements in existing products or needs.
3. Look for feature improvements and adding features.
4. Translate some new technology or invention into a useful thing.
5. Dream up a million-dollar idea out of thin air.

One common feature of these approaches is the process of iteration, trial and error, testing and retesting solutions until you are either tired of trying or out of budget or time. Every design can be improved.

Product: Serengeti Sunglasses
Designer: Tucker Viemeister
Company: Smart Design
Client: Corning Glassworks
Year: 1984

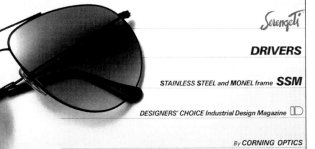

Serengeti
DRIVERS
STAINLESS STEEL and MONEL frame **SSM**
DESIGNERS' CHOICE Industrial Design Magazine
By **CORNING OPTICS**

Designing consumer products must be a challenge, given the high volumes and design constraints.
No, that's an advantage. I want to design stuff that a lot of people can get their hands on! If you mean it's hard to create general products that appeal to a wide range of customers, even that isn't so hard, for two reasons: (1) there are large and small sizes of target consumer groups, and (2) everyone's a consumer, so all projects are for consumers.

Tell me about the latest project you are working on.
We are working on a project where we have a totally blank canvas to do anything we want, any where in the world, so long as it benefits the company's profits! Almost anything could do that; all they want is innovation! It's like a student project, only I get a lot of help (and get paid for it!). We are looking at small things like packaging and big things like the vehicles they drive!

Product: Phat Farm
Designers: Henry Myerberg,
Tucker Viemeister
Company: Smart Design and HMA
Client: Phat Farm
Year: 1997

Product: National Zoo
Designers: Lance Wyman, Bill Cannan, Brian Flahive, Tucker Viemeister
Company: Wyman and Cannan
Client: Smithsonian
Year: 1975
Photo: Lance Wyman

How do you go about designing something that seems to be about function only?
First, I think the aesthetics of a product are part of the function: good-looking stuff is more attractive to users and therefore works better (at the very least, in their own mind). Second, I look at the problem up close and from a distance in many ways to solve it and to improve the solutions. I observe people who are or will be using the things. Usually I make a matrix of needs and solutions to see where opportunities might be. Then in a loose, empirical way I prioritize. I sketch some ideas (with a pencil and paper), make rough mockups of the best ideas, maybe do some computer work, talk to manufacturers, and go back to the users again.

How do you test your designs? Do you make a lot of prototypes?
I start by testing them on myself; then I bring in other people. You have to make mistakes in order to make innovations.

Do you get to meet lots of types of consumers? Do they influence the design?
I try to meet people because I need them to help me with the design. Consumer testing is a bummer when our design is not good enough (we failed) or when consumer testing picks one we don't like (we fail in another way)!

Do you do a lot of research?

You need to do some research in order to create a good design. We do designcentric research: market surveys, user studies, ergonomic studies. Designers need to feel what users are going to want.

How do you design?

I think, scribble, discuss, then make mockups, both digital and real, and test them out, both functionally and aesthetically. I love to work in the shop, but it's great to have computers to finalize the designs. The trick is to integrate all the media in a way that makes the final results the best.

You have also designed interiors. Is the process different than for designing products?

It's the same process, but with different parameters. It's a different kind of space, but it's still three-dimensional, it still has to be desirable, and it still has to feel good and function.

What's in your future? What do you want to design?

I'm looking for a car project because they are big and a place where form is king!

What's in the future for industrial design?

Industrial design in the future is going to be less about just making products and more about facilitating the communication between the user and the producer. In other words, we are talented translators.

Eventually, I hope, everyone will be his or her own designer. It's the ultimate democracy! Everyone is smart and able to express personal talent to the max.

What is your favorite design? Why?

I like my Apple Power Book G4 because it is simple and plain.

What is your least favorite design? Why?

Any SUV, because SUVs are designed to be big with no consideration for form, community, or ecology.

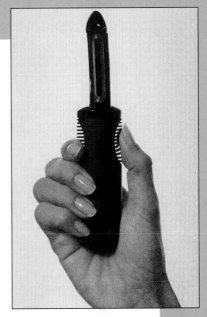

Product: Oxo Good Grip Peeler
Designers: Davin Stowell, Tucker Viemeister, Michael Calahan, Dan Formosa, Stephen Russak, Stephan Allendorf
Company: Smart Design
Client: OXO
Date: 1991

Product: Smart Mixer
Designers: Tucker Viemeister, Scott Henderson
Company: Smart Design
Client: Cuisinart

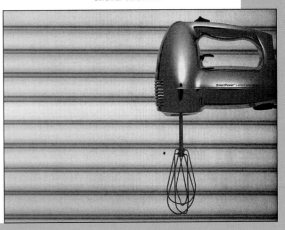

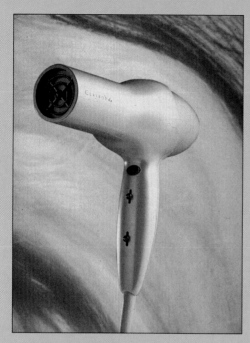

How do you work? In collaboration? Alone?
Collaboration has two advantages: (1) bouncing ideas off other people causes the ideas to grow, and (2) the other person checks your ideas, giving the process more objectivity. But you also have to work things out alone because deep thought is not possible with the distraction of another person.

Can you sum up your design philosophy in one word? Why?
Beauty: because you said only one word.
Everything: Either life is futile, or we can make it better. I think we can (no one else will).

Product: Aero Hair Dryer
Designers: Tucker Viemeister, David Peschel
Company: Smart Design
Client: Clairol, Remington
Year: 1995

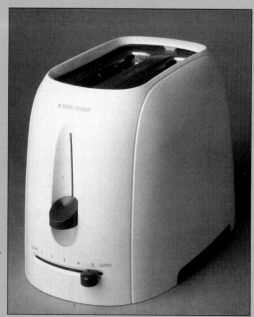

Product: Metropolitan Toaster
Designer: Tucker Viemeister, Tom Dair
Company: Smart Design
Client: Black and Decker
Year: 1992
Photo: Tucker Viemeister

Self-Respect

DESIGNER: PETER BRESSLER
Title: Principal
Firm Name: Bressler Group, Inc.
Location: Philadelphia, Pennsylvania

Why did you start your own company?
During school, I suspect, we all fantasize about having our own firms. My relatives encouraged me to complete the design of my senior thesis, the Standup Wheelchair, and find a licensee for manufacture. Three years later the chair was licensed, but I was left with $20,000 in debt. So I started my business in 1972 with huge debt, no contacts, no clients, a chamber of commerce directory, and the telephone. I would not recommend this as a good plan for starting a consulting business. Fortunately it got better.

What was your first successful product? The telescope?
Success can be measured in numerous ways. I consider the Standup Wheelchair successful because of its positive reception by the market, but it was not a financial success.

I certainly wish I had had a royalty on the Edmunds Astroscan Telescope. The original market projections were for 2,500 units per year. It has sold an average of 10,000 units per year since 1976 and was selected as a Consumer Reports best choice for Christmas in 2001 at three times the original sales price. These are not large numbers from the consumer product perspective, but in the amateur telescope market they are significant.

You have designed for the U.S. Postal Service. Is designing systems different than designing products? Why?
The work we did in mail-handling systems was actually for Opex Corporation. This work is not significantly different from designing consumer products but can require more objective rigor, compromise, and a broader perspective. It is extremely gratifying to complete a piece of equipment, test it, and find that the solutions you designed really do make it easier, more

Product: Standup Wheelchair
Designer: Peter Bressler
Year: 1972

Product: Edmunds Astroscan
Telescope
Designer: Peter Bressler
Year: 1976

comfortable, and safer for people who use the equipment ten hours a day, six days a week.

You have been involved in industrial design for years. Has the design field changed? What is different today?

The field has been changing constantly, as it must, as I entered it in the late 1960s. There are, of course, the cycles of interest: human factors application, design for disabilities, clever manufacturing processes, unique materials applications, ecological awareness, design for recycling, design for reuse, user needs definition, visual semantics, styling, visual communication, interface architecture—each in its turn adding value at yet another level to the work we do.

What has changed that troubles me is that the design profession in its fervor to educate and emulate business has embraced some of business's less worthy qualities. The reason for becoming an industrial designer, when I entered the field, was to contribute to society by solving real problems and adding greater functionality and beauty to the artifacts that contribute to the quality of life. Over the past ten to fifteen years, more and more firms have been taken over by people whose highest priority is not contribution to society but contribution to their bottom line. It is frustrating to work within an ethical framework and find oneself competing against firms that offer superficial work for free or for half its minimum value. This kind of unprofessional practice is in direct conflict with the IDSA Code of Ethics.

What goes into designing a successful product?

It is just as easy to design an unsuccessful product as a successful one. Designing an extraordinarily successful product, in which we have a pretty good track record, requires something extra. It requires understanding the user and the use environment of the product at an empathic level. It requires feeling not only the physical but the emotional needs of the person who is buying and using the product. It requires stepping back from the rules you've been given and

Product: MSI/Radioshack Digital Tire Gauge
Designer: Peter Bressler

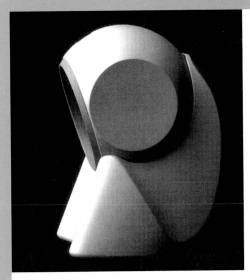

Product: Polk M3 Speakers
Designer: Peter Bressler

asking "what else?" It then requires being able to include that something extra in a form that visually communicates itself to the user. The Polk M3 speakers had it. They expected to sell 50,000 and sold 250,000 pairs in eighteen months. The Southco Sealed Lever Latch had it. They projected 5,000 per year and have sold 100,000 per year.

Do you do a lot of research? Focus groups?

Yes, we have always done as much research as possible on our projects. That comes from my 1960s RISD (Rhode Island School of Design) training. Even when we haven't quoted a separate research phase, we do something to stimulate the ideation process and substantiate the results. We do visual vocabulary research, competitive benchmarking, observational and ethnographic focus groups, and both qualitative and quantitative analysis. We developed a focus group process we call "group visualization," where a designer draws what the attendees say they want. This provides a visual interpretation of the words that have already been agreed to by the group and can be very powerful. Also, we find research plays an important role in revealing conflicts that must be resolved through design innovation to create large and small added values to most of the products we develop.

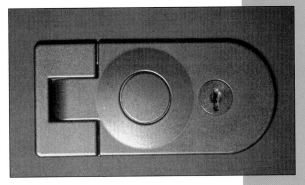

Product: Southco Sealed Lever
Designer: Peter Bressler

Do you have a few words of wisdom for people starting their own design business?

1. Don't start as I did, from scratch, with no money or contacts.
2. Try to remember that most of what is needed to be successful in business could not be taught by your design school.
3. Have enough money not only to begin but to sustain yourself.
4. Remember that most firms fail within the first five years.
5. Know yourself well enough to understand whether you have the right personality for self-promotion, marketing, and selling.

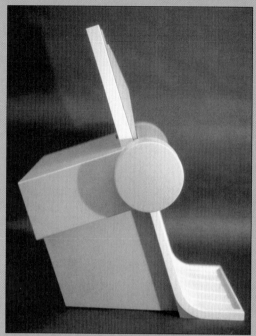

What is it like to own and run a small company?

Had I started the firm under different circumstances, my perception of the role of owner would be different. In the best of times, I love it when we are all feeling good about the results of a project, when we win a design award or I can give out profit-sharing after a good year. I get excited when we receive an over-the-transom call from a big-name company. I have begun to enjoy the challenge of designing an organization and planning its future. I hate not being able to make a payroll on time, not being able to afford equipment, software, or people we want when we want them, having to fire or lay someone off.

Can you sum up your design philosophy in one word?

Self-respect.

Product: Vidar XR-12 X-ray Scanner
Designers: John Coleman,
Peter Bressler
Creative Director: Peter Bressler
Client: Vidar Incorporated
Year: 1990

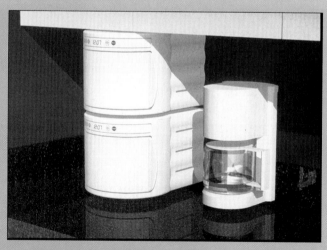

Product: Stackable Rotary Microwave Ovens
Designers: Peter Byar, Peter Bressler
Creative Director: Peter Bressler
Client: Microwave Research Group
Year: 1995

Design Fast, Think About It Later!

DESIGNER: PAUL METAXATOS

Title: Design Manager
Firm Name: Proteus Design
Location: Boston, Massachusetts

How do you work?

We research the market first and understand the problem from the point of view of the retail buyer and consumer. Once you understand the market needs, it is easy to structure the design process to fulfill them. We conduct store audits and Internet research as well as formalized research such as mall intercepts, one-on-one interviews, and focus groups to get the information we need.

We then conduct a series of internal brainstorming sessions to produce as many ideas as possible with the intent of sifting through those ideas to find the best ones for the project. Our intent is always to deliver a proprietary protectable invention as well as progressive styling and solid ergonomics. Once we have directions we like, we realize the solution through mockups, computer-generated databases, renderings, and, finally, prototypes. The end of the process always includes testing the solution with consumers.

Is there a product you designed that makes you particularly happy?

The UPS DIAD III was a project I really enjoyed developing. I see the drivers using the product every day, and they have told me the new design has made their job easier.

When you are designing, who finally says "this is it"? The client? You?

I typically lock a direction down as quickly as possible, as the majority of time with most projects is spent on the details.

Product: UPS Diad III
Designers: Paul Metaxatos, Group Four Design Staff, UPS, Motorola
Creative Director: Paul Metaxatos
Company: Group Four Design
Client: UPS
Year: 1998
Photo: Group Four Design

Product: Honeywell Warm Mist Humidifier
Designers: Paul Metaxatos, John Shaffield, Steffen Koury, Meral Middleton, Honeywell, and Proteus Design Engineering Staff
Creative Director: Paul Metaxatos
Company: Proteus Design
Client: Honeywell
Year: 2002
Photo: Proteus Design

Product: Honeywell Ceramic Heaters
Designers: Paul Metaxatos, John Shaffield, Steffen Koury, Meral Middleton, Honeywell, and Proteus Design Engineering Staff
Creative Director: Paul Metaxatos
Company: Proteus Design
Client: Honeywell
Year: 2002
Photo: Proteus Design

Do you have a favorite client or design experience?
Hunter Douglas window fashions is one of my favorite clients, mostly because my contact there is a brilliant inventor. We have great synergy, and it's a real pleasure to work with him.

When you are designing, how do you work? Do you mock things up in your shop?
I like to understand the category and competition first. Then we can start to generate rough concepts and develop mockups to assess size and form issues. Once we have focused on a direction, we realize the form as a hard model and engineering database.

Who are your clients?
Currently our clients are mostly large corporations like Baldwin, Hunter Douglas, Polaroid, and Salton, although we occasionally work with inventors. One of our most recent large projects was a new design language for Honeywell. Once we developed a look, we developed a line of humidifiers and heaters. The designs are important because they increased our client's bottom line by 30 percent, improved the perception of the brand to retailers and consumers, and helped them sell the company. Aesthetically, the designs changed the paradigm about these types of products.

What inspired you to be a designer?
I have always been interested in how things work. As kids, my brother and I disassembled every product we could find and usually got punished for it when my dad came home!

Can you sum up your design philosophy in one word?
Design fast, think about it later!

Listen

DESIGNER: GEORGE SCHMIDT

Title: President
Firm Name: George Schmidt, Inc.
Location: Douglaston, New York

How did you discover industrial design?
I discovered industrial design when I entered the Fisher Body Craftsmans Guild car design competition when I was about fourteen. I won awards all three years I entered, but in retrospect I believe they probably gave all entrants some sort of recognition. In addition, my sister was dating an industrial design student at Pratt. I was at Brooklyn Technical High School heading for a career in engineering, but I changed my mind on seeing his work.

How do you work?
When we start a project, we have open-ended conversations about what we need to do. We do a great deal of scroll sketching and have periodic pin-up reviews of concepts. Most of the time we tend to cross-fertilize our ideas until we refine our thinking to a manageable number of concepts. We then create presentation renderings, but in some cases we go directly to three-dimensional sketch models, which we call form studies. If that old saying about a picture being worth a thousand words is true, a model must be worth a thousand pictures. We maintain our own model shop and do most of our own three-dimensional work, although with the advent of computerized modeling, some of the more complex work is done elsewhere.

Pro Steel collection of Sabatier stainless-steel cutlery for the Excel Group, 1999

How do you create a family of products?

Aside from the obvious elements such as color, materials, and graphic treatments, a designer needs to reflect the gestalt (for lack of a better description) of the client's company. We did a lot of work for Salton years ago, and their products' persona was a reflection of the personality of its founder, Lew Salton, a man of sophistication, humor, and intelligence who required those characteristics in his product offerings. In our work for Helen of Troy (Revlon and Vidal Sassoon personal care products) we attempted to create a unified image for a line of products through form, giving each element a shape that related to the rest of the collection.

Product: Adagio line of cast-metal bath wall hardware (clockwise from top left: tumbler/toothbrush holder, toilet tissue holder, 24" towel bar, single hook)
Client: Creative Bath Products
Year: 2002

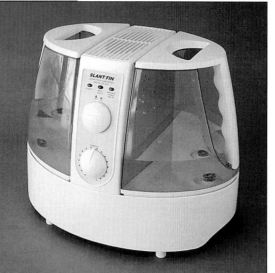

Product: GF-220 Germ-Free Humidifier
Client: Slant/Fin Corporation
Description: Features ultraviolet light in combination with a boiler to purify the water supply
Year: 2002

When you are designing, who finally says "this is it"?

More often than not it is the client, but a good designer must be prepared to advocate on behalf of his design and convince a client that it is indeed the best solution possible and deserves validation. Just think of what Daniel Libeskind had to go through to convince the jury that his was indeed the best design for rebuilding of the World Trade Center site.

When you are designing, how do you work? Do you mock things up in your shop?

We have become proficient in creating quick form studies out of paper, plaster, wood, and foam, which allows us to present our initial design ideas in three dimensions. I have found this an important communication tool because so many people have difficulty reading drawings. But more importantly, the sketch model allows me to clarify my own thinking before presenting a design solution. We have made a few additions to our home over the past few years, and each time I have made a model of the planned changes so I can clarify my thinking and better explain the proposed changes to my wife and sons.

What's in your future? What do you want to design?

I'd like to turn my attention to more personal products. We've done a few stainless-steel flatware patterns recently, and I find that a calming and personal form of expression. We have done some acrylic and melamine tableware, and that too has an intimacy I find gratifying. I am also passionate about gardening, a discipline I find to be more and more a metaphor for life.

What's in the future for industrial design?

Technology, but I say that with mixed feelings. I see young people coming out of design school with all sorts of computer capabilities but unable to draw and express themselves. I have always thought of industrial design as an art form in the same way we conceive of architecture as art. But as technology becomes more and more dominant, the idiosyncrasy of personality is being replaced by the homogeneity of the computer. One can hope that once we have conquered the machine or once it becomes more human, it will be relegated to its appropriate position of tool, not driver.

Product: Mariko collection of stainless-steel flatware
Client: Gingko International
Year: 2001

Is it fun and exciting to see your work in use? Are you critical of it? What would you change?

Bringing a well-designed product to market is a bit like bringing a child into the world (please do not share this with my wife!): a few moments of inspiration and nine months of development followed by a lot of screaming and a good deal of pain. But if you did it correctly you have made a real contribution to our world.

What is product design?

Giving form, reason, and personality to the inanimate.

What is your most successful design? Why?

I hope my most successful design is yet to come, but if one measures success in numbers, it would be a whistling glass kettle I designed over twenty-five years ago for Gemco-Ware. It's still selling about a million units a year.

Product: Whistling Glass Kettle
Client: Gemco-Ware
Year: 1975

What is your favorite design? Why?
Most favorite designs would include my stacking stainless-steel
cookware line designed for Cuisine Cookware and the Mariko
flatware pattern I did for Ginkgo International.

Where do you get your ideas?
I enjoy walking through department and specialty stores to see
what's around. I go to trade shows like the International
Housewares Show or the Tabletop Show to see what's going on in
new products. It's important to be aware of what other people are
doing and which companies pay serious attention to design.

Can you sum up your design philosophy in one word? Why?
Listen. Because if you don't listen, you can't hear, and if you can't
hear, you won't know what's going on around you.

Why Followed by How

DESIGNER: GIANFRANCO ZACCAI

Title: President
Firm Name: Design Continuum
Location: West Newton, Massachusetts

How did you discover industrial design?

As a freshman in the Syracuse architecture program, I saw all these models of things that were part of everyday life. I had never thought about anyone actually designing those things. After I earned a degree in industrial design, I got one in architecture; the two disciplines inform each other quite well.

How do you work?

There are two basic, connected notions in our work process, starting with the supposition that we don't know much, even if something is familiar to us. We step back and look at the reality from different perspectives, from the point of view of others with different values and different sensibilities.

Design is not something just one person does. Design is informed, it evolves over time, and many people contribute to the process simultaneously: engineers, industrial designers, interaction designers, graphic designers, software people, all stepping back together. The entire team is responsible for the overall experience or result, each individual contributing specific skills not only to make magic happen but also to stimulate one another. We also involve real people as much as possible in our design research process.

What do you design?

Anything I can get my hands on! My start as a designer was in medical products because it represented a wonderful space where technology and humanity meet, an area filled with emotional and critical needs. Working in that environment taught me that experts don't have all the answers, and really understanding the dynamics of real-life situations comes by spending time in hospitals and labs, with patients, doctors, nurses, surgeons, and technicians.

Product: Affymetrix GenChip Scanner 3000
Designers: Allan Cameron, Kevin Young, Sebastian Petry, Scott Chapps, Peter Bates
Client: Affymetrix, Santa Clara, CA
Year: 2002

Product: Oster In2itive Blender
Designers: Allan Cameron, Kevin Young, David Malina, Ann Sullivan, Allan Mudd, Aaron Oppenheimer, Cordy Swope, and Cyan Godfrey and Dylan Akinele (Refac Design, New York)
Client: Sunbeam Corporation
Photo: Sal Gracefa
Year: 2001

We're now involved in many areas, including sporting goods, consumer electronics, and transportation products. We justify the fun of design by reminding ourselves that if we continuously designed the same things, we wouldn't be stimulated by the serendipitous events and ideas that come from experimenting in many areas. It's stimulating to learn about new things all the time, to immerse yourself in different worlds. Diverse knowledge—the cross-fertilization of stimuli—brings value to your designs.

Our idea is not to design things in design magazines but to come up with an elegantly simple solution to a complex series of problems. Products, like living things, go through an evolutionary process; it is ultimately survival of the fittest. To get to the essence of an idea and how the essence is embodied in the ultimate design, a designer must cultivate an understanding of the external forces and internal technology involved. Hopefully, that creates things that don't look like we "designed" them, and when people encounter them, they say, "Isn't this great!"

Take us through a typical product development process.

1. Determine the client's purpose and understand the objectives; then question whether that purpose is appropriate enough.

2. Step back and shift perspectives. What is the essence of the product? What does it expect to deliver and what can we do better? What is the purpose of the product? A tool, or a toy? Both? Can one become the other? What are the alternatives, variations, mutations?

3. Increasingly, a lot of our work deals with doing empathic research, where the purpose is seeking innovation driven by people, not technology, where product development is not predetermined, not "Can you design this chair for us?" but rather "We have a seating problem." We then ask, "Why are the end-users sitting in the first place? What characteristics define a really good sitting experience?"

4. Then we make that research tangible to our client, they become excited about the prospect of the solution, and we build enthusiasm within our own organization among those who will contribute their own creativity to the process.

5. From brainstorming sessions, we take ideas that seem viable, and by trial and error create mockups, simulations, and models. Testing them, we make mistakes faster than anyone else. We gather more information; we repeat the process until the idea is refined, until we have the sense that we have done the right thing. The superfluous ideas fall off, the essential are embedded, and the result has poetry and integrity.

Product: Coleman Charcoal Grill
Designers: Marc Bates, Sebastian Petry, Jim Wilson
Client: Sunbeam Corporation
Year: 1999
Photo: S. Michael Brzoza

Do you have a favorite client or design experience?

The research division of Herman Miller, a company with high ethical standards, was asked to examine design for the aging population. They conducted research with gerontologists and over 100 subjects and determined five key elements necessary for people to be independent in their own homes: personal hygiene, food preparation, long-term sitting, sleeping, and materials handling.

I was presented with this open-ended problem statement: Explore personal hygiene that would allow people to live independently in their own homes. The Metaform Project, as it was called, gave us an opportunity to create a universally appealing design solution that made a significant difference in peoples' lives. Coincidentally, at the time we were working on this, my own father developed severe health problems in his eighties. I could see him struggling, and I could also see his need for dignity. It was a great opportunity to work with him and to have an intimate glimpse into why many products designed to help the elderly or disabled are not accepted.

What's in your future?

I am interested in the fusion of architectural and industrial design principles, not from the standpoint of the home as an art statement but the home as a space for living life, sharing moments.

Product: PediSedate
Designers: Allan Cameron, Kevin Young, Thorben Neu, Scott Chapps, David Chastain, John MacNeil, Geoffrey Hart, MD
Client: Elliott C. Kulakowshi, Ph.D., Director, Research and Development, Albert Einstein Healthcare Network Corporation
Year: 2002
Photo: S. Michael Brzoza

You have written about the poetry of design. Are there examples of designs you have done that you find poetic?
Very few. I always see flaws, especially in my own work. I have an easier time seeing poetry in others' work. One of the most poetic solutions for me is the original design of the Vespa. My father had one, and I remember holding onto him; it was like riding on Superman's cape! The Vespa became so successful because it was an aeronautical engineer's cross-fertilized idea: unisex design, frameless, natural elegance. A symbol of freedom and joie de vivre that still resonates, the Vespa is a practical and enduring fusion of fashion, technology, and lifestyle.

What is your most successful design? Why?
Define success. The Reebok pump sneakers were the most successful design because of the sales volume they generated. A successful medical design I did a long time ago is still on the market. The product set a standard of reference and transformed the company.

Can you sum up your design philosophy in one word? Why?

Clarity

DESIGNER: TAD TOULIS

Title: Founder
Firm Name: designRAW
Location: Boston, Massachusetts

How did you discover industrial design?
As a kid I wanted to be a comic book artist or, failing that, a spaceman. Somewhere along the line a family friend gave me a book about Raymond Loewy detailing his work for NASA. I realized I was more interested in making and drawing spaceships than being a spaceman.

How do you work?
I try to find a challenging angle to confront myself with. Generally, I don't communicate to anyone what this angle is until I'm confident it is leading somewhere. I first stumbled on this process when I was working on sketches for a CRT monitor. I tried using one radius everywhere combined with extruded silhouettes. The client didn't choose it, but it helped get me enthused. Increasingly, as a result of the work we do with RAW, the story becomes a bigger part of project definition. I like to start with ideas and stories. The best method for me is to have a clear idea that almost renders itself; then the task becomes getting out of its way.

Sketching is important, but the emphasis should be the content of the sketch or what the sketch is

Product: Cleanscape for Whirlpool
Designer: Tad Toulis
Year: 2001

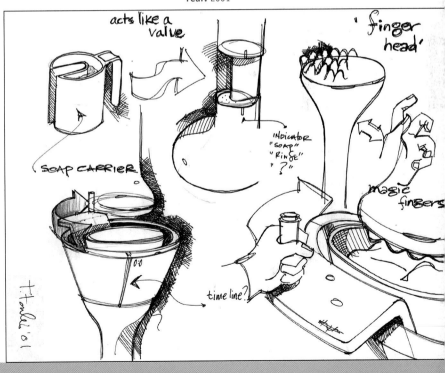

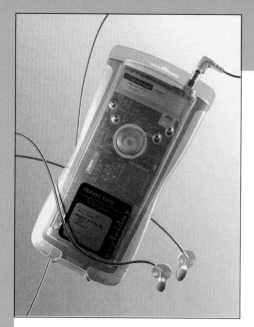

Product: Milan Dialogs
Designer: DesignRAW
Year: 2000

communicating. Given that most products are three-dimensional, a two-dimensional sketch communicates some qualities, but not all. Placing too much emphasis on a graphic representation of a design is a misleading process. Sometimes when dealing with clients this can be a place where miscommunication happens.

Tell me about RAW. What is it? Why is it?
DesignRAW got its start during a year I lived in Milan. I visited the *salone di mobile* that year and was impressed by the *salone satellite*, the pavilion dedicated to younger designers. Upon my return to San Francisco I approached two colleagues about collaborating on an event for the *salone*. Over time, that group expanded to include eight (now seven) people. The work we do is collaborative, and while it actively seeks to avoid typecasting, its goal is to explore social issues using design as a medium.

DesignRAW is a funny thing—not quite art, not quite product design. The result is that we are a bit of a bastard child.

Do you do a lot of research?
For mass-produced work, focus groups, materials, and processes are integral parts of the process. Co-opting some aspects of this process can help you greatly in the politicized atmosphere of product development. You are talking about hundreds of thousands of dollars in tools and more for marketing. It's understandable that clients want to remove as much risk from the process as they can. The trick is to avoid having the design become victimized by the process. Design is a creative process and, as such, risk must be held close at hand. You can't hit a home run by preparing to bunt. Validating a design to death is to be avoided. At a focus group you need smart people asking the questions and smart people evaluating the answers; if not, you often end up throwing out the good along with the bad. At the same time, I find myself at odds with diva designers who feel entitled

Product: Sony Home Monitor
Designer: Sand Box Studios
Year: 1998

to take liberties with their clients' resources. The best argument for a design is a designer who can see the whole picture, balance the forces, and still achieve the vision.

How do you design?

Listening. Hearing. Thinking. Reflection. Sketching. Mockups. Models.

Is designing fun? What makes you want to design products?

The only times I have found design not fun is when I am dealing with groups who want to boil the process down to a science. To make a great thing requires a fair amount of the unpredictable—the inspired.

What's in the future for industrial design?

The future of design is not that different from its past. The human desire to solve problems will persist. The one fear I have for design is that it will become wholly co-opted by advertisers and marketing groups to a point where it loses its own potential. I often see analogies between design and other commercial arts. To me, the core of industrial design is a bit like that of the independent film culture.

Product: Service as Product
Designer: Jeff Hoeffer, LUNAR Design
Year: 1999

Do you have a few words of wisdom for people starting out in the design business?

No opportunity is too small. Almost every design project can teach you something if you proceed with an open mind. The one constant I have learned is that the more of myself I put into my process, the better and more stimulating the work becomes. One must learn the elements of an objective foundation in design, but the overwhelming balance of the process is subjective.

Who are your clients?

At designRAW, our clients tend to be design galleries and furniture fairs. One notable exception is the project we recently completed with Whirlpool Europe. Whirlpool's design director contacted me about getting RAW involved in a design program they were undertaking to investigate the future of garment care. Our point of departure was this challenge: What does *clean* mean and, by extension, what does *clean clothing* mean? Setting up the design opportunity in this way helped us immediately avoid attempting to redesign a washing machine. Our final solution incorporated an iconic design with an elegant solution: Cleanscape.

In this instance, as with most of our work, we tried to balance an understated physical design with a rich user scenario. This is the strength of my work and the work we do as designRAW. If the designs we create can help access ideas in people's heads, then I think we've designed something valid.

What are you working on now?
I recently started working with the advanced concepts group of a telecommunication company that has the resources and the corporate mandate to explore how interface, product design, and technology can be woven together with user attitudes to explore design issues in a way that has incredible breadth.

Can you sum up your design philosophy in one word? Why?
Clarity. I think good product design is approachable and eminently understandable. Beauty comes across in its execution.

Product: Cleanscape for Whirlpool
Designer: Franco Lombardi
Year: 2002

You Can Never Be Too Simple

DESIGNER: MARK DZIERSK

Title: Vice President of Design
Firm Name: Herbst LaZar Bell, Inc.
Location: Chicago, Illinois

How did you discover industrial design?
At age seventeen I watched an eight-part PBS program on Leonardo da Vinci and decided that the modern-day equivalent would be my career. A couple of months later, a local high school held an art day and I watched an industrial designer conducting a rendering demo. That sealed the deal.

Do you have a favorite client or design experience?
Tenex, a company that makes desktop office products, asked me to reinvent the Rolodex. The X file, Tenex's Rolodex, is perhaps my favorite product I designed. It is simple and based on strong geometry. The X shape plays off the heavy x type in the Tenex logo, scattering these strong brand images throughout an office. And, most importantly, the product increases the speed by which a user can find information via a patented multitiered card design. I have two X files on my desk and I use them every day.

Is it fun and exciting to see your work in use?
It's a great feeling when someone hands me a Kodak camera I designed or I see people using the Suave and Caress bottles we designed.

I established our Vision Program, which focuses on inventing/ picturing the future now. One Vision project is Zuzu, a PDA with leaves that are plucked and worn as jewelry, then returned to a home base to download and reenergize from digital dirt stored in its base. The metaphors are about nature and drawing power from the sun. To upgrade, you "repot" it.

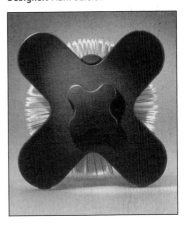

Product: Tenex X File, rotary address card organizer
Designer: Mark Dziersk

Product: Unilever Caress, Body Wash structural packaging
Designers: Jason Martin, Mark Dziersk
Photo: Tom Petroff

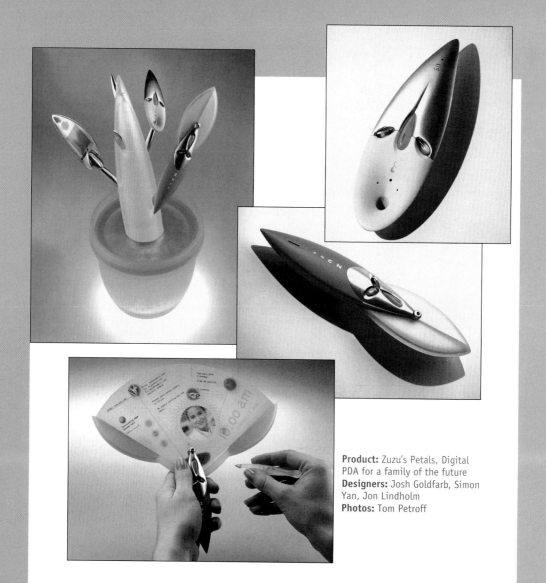

Product: Zuzu's Petals, Digital PDA for a family of the future
Designers: Josh Goldfarb, Simon Yan, Jon Lindholm
Photos: Tom Petroff

Is the design of consumer products a particular challenge, given high volumes and constraints?
Charles Eames once famously said, "Without constraint there is no design." I consider those challenges the only ones that matter.

What's in the future for industrial design?
Technological advances are the most import future issue for design. One day there will be a chip in everything, from a water glass that alerts a waiter that a refill is needed to wrist-worn computers. The more technical complexity is involved, the more restraint is required to make usable things for all people.

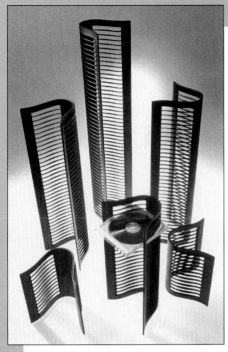

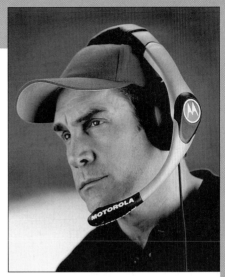

Product: Motorola NFL Headset
Designers: John Hartman, Jason Billig, Elliot Hsu
Photo: Tom Petroff

Product: Tenex CD Tower
Designer: Mark Dziersk

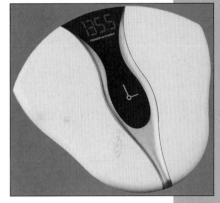

What is product design?
The most fun you can have at work.

What is your most successful design?
The first Kodak single-use camera, because it is the highest-volume camera ever manufactured. It replaced an overpackaged product with an almost completely recycled solution where Kodak uses the last camera and its parts to make the next camera. Simple one-button use, universal in many ways, and everyone has used one at one time.

Product: Sunbeam Scales
Designers: Monique Chatterjee, Elliot Hsu, Greg Holderfield, Randy Bell,
Photo: Sunbeam

What is your favorite design that never got made?
El Diablo! It was a fire starter I made in the shape of the devil. Go figure.

Can you sum up your design philosophy in a few words?
You can never be too simple.

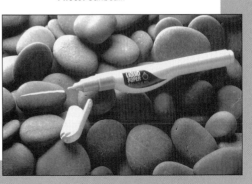

Product: Liquid Paper Guppy Pen
Designers: John Hartman, Jason Billig, Elliot Hsu
Photo: Tom Petroff

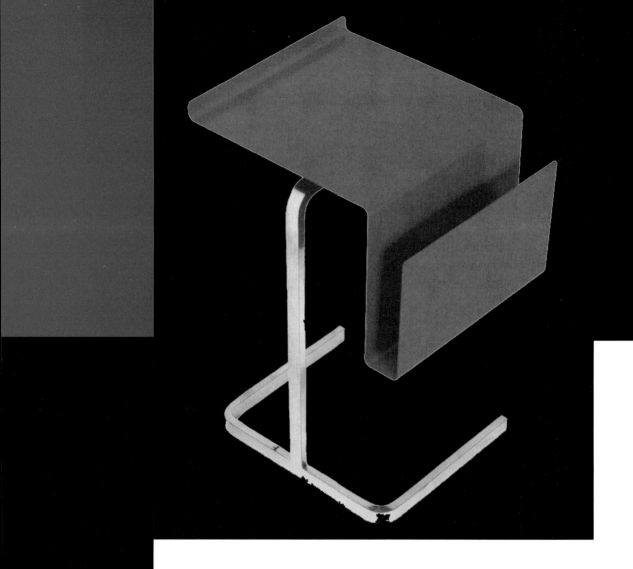

Chapter Five

Furniture

When you sit in a chair you probably don't think about your lumbar being supported, but the chair's designer did. Everything you sat on today, starting with the toilet bowl seat, designers contributed to. Seats on buses, trains, and airplanes and in theaters and offices are all designed—and more likely than not, by an industrial designer. Furniture design ranges from the mundane folding chair to the fantastic lounge chair. We use furniture a lot. We store stuff in it, write on it, and sleep in it. Industrial designers are responsible for designing furniture that's easy to use, delightful to look at, and affordable. This area of design challenges the designer to create products that touch many aspects of our lives. We identify our homes and ourselves through furnishings. Styling furniture for many points of view, from traditional to modern, is just one of the exciting parts of furniture design.

As I spoke with furniture designers, I was reminded of teaching a group of children at the Cooper-Hewitt, National Design Museum. I asked them to build a stool from six boards, all of the same size. Many variations were possible. The children were quite proud of the stools they built, and they sat proudly on them. Then I asked them to paint the stools. As they were painting, I asked them why they chose the colors they did. The replies usually involved another person. My sister likes blue; my mother likes green and yellow. The children were changing the stools to suit someone else's taste or style. They were making the stool for someone else. It became a gift. Designers aren't much different; they create furniture for someone else—although Mark Goetz says one of the reasons he designs furniture is that he would like to own it himself.

Furniture designers work in many ways—as independent designers, freelance designers, corporate employees, and in design offices that practice in many fields. Probably the most famous independent designers are Ray and Charles Eames, noted for their work for Herman Miller. Their classic chair designs are seen everywhere from airports to schools to offices. You have probably sat in one of their chairs, unaware that it was designed by anyone of importance.

Charles Eames and Eero Saarinen, more than any other designers, are responsible for the modern style we all associate with the 1950s. Their furniture is collectible, and rare pieces sell for thousands of dollars. In 1946 the

Museum of Modern Art in New York ran a competition for low-cost modern design, which Eames and Saarinen won. Their designs sent a shock wave through the design community, mainly because of their introduction of new materials such as fiberglass and bent plywood. The new materials helped them design new and innovative forms that conjured a new dialog between consumers and manufacturers. They also created a new freedom for designers, who until that competition had mostly worked for corporations and churned out designs reminiscent of historical styles. Eames and Saarinen opened a new approach to design and to ideas about what designers could and could not do. In the 1970s, with Ettore Sottsass's adventures in Memphis, furniture design was once again stood on its ear.

Most designers, when asked the question "who are your heroes?" will answer Charles Eames and Eero Saarinen. They established a way of working on furniture that persists today. They built full-size working prototypes that anyone could sit in and test for comfort and appearance. Furniture designers work this way. They might build scale models of an idea, but very soon they will construct a working prototype. In schools that teach furniture design, many students have their first experience of designing and building the real thing. Unlike the design of electronic products, for example, which is often prohibitively expensive, furniture design allows the designer to experience the product firsthand.

Many furniture designers work alone or with a small group of associates. Furniture design is about testing ideas quickly and seeing if the idea works or not, getting responses from many individuals and groups, and modifying and improving the idea. Some designers start out with quick mockups of the seat and back of a chair, trying to establish the right relationship between them for comfort and posture. After this relationship is established, the design of the supporting pieces begins.

Research plays an important role in furniture design; many large furniture companies employ full-time market researchers, materials researchers, and manufacturing researchers whose job is to find an edge or new method of manufacture. Furniture designers fill many of these roles and often are searching for new ways to manufacture furniture.

The many kinds of furniture designers and manufacturers range from entre-preneurial designers who start their own manufacturing company to large corporations that produce modern and classic furniture. Designers can find opportunities everywhere. Working independently is the dream of many fur-niture designers, who yearn to design and manufacture their own work. But many designers work quite happily in large corporations designing lines of furniture and accessories.

Personal

DESIGNER: MARK GOETZ

Title: Founder
Firm Name: TZ Design, Inc.
Location: New York City

When did you know you wanted to be a product designer?
I knew I wanted to be a furniture designer when I was nineteen
and took a course in drafting and design at California State
Teachers College in Pennsylvania.

Why furniture?
I like designing something I can make full size. I can control the
whole process from design to manufacture. There's also the
immediate gratification of sitting on something I've made. I want
to create something that people will remember me by.

What is your favorite design?
The Esperanto Chair. I started looking at
the oldest chairs I could find from Egypt
and Greece, and I discovered some of the
most beautiful designs. I wanted to see
if I could make something as beautiful.
At the same time I was working on a
table, and I wanted it to evoke the most
modern object I could think of—the
sleek whiteness of the Concorde.
Designing both products—one ancient,
one contemporary—stands out as a peak
experience of what I want to do in
design.

When do you do your best work?
When I work with companies, the best
experiences are when someone with a
point of view like an art director or
editor is involved. When I was doing the

Product: Esperanto Chair
Design: Mark Goetz
Courtesy of Bernhardt Design

Product: Claris Seating and Table
Design: Mark Goetz
Courtesy of Bernhardt Design

sofa at Herman Miller, the guy who directed the design was a fan of classic Herman Miller furniture. The reason I couldn't have gone down that road without him was he was steering the design to be compatible with their classics. The sofa is much better because of his involvement.

My friend Jerry at Bernhart is a great editor. He trusts me to come up with a design, and I trust him to make changes. The client and the designer must be mutually trusting.

Why do you choose to work alone?
I want to be involved in the design, not run a business. I love the process of thinking about the design from concept to reality. I start with an idea, but I think about it a long time before I sketch it. Then I make little sketches to capture the feeling. Once I've got that, I make larger sketches to show a client. From there I sketch full-size with a large magic marker to get the feeling again. Then we draw the chair in CAD and make a full-size mockup.

Can you sum up your design philosophy in one word?
Personal. Design needs to be personal. I try to make furniture people will be attracted to and attached to. I try to bring a sense of style to the products I design. I know some people do not like the idea of style, but I think style is very important. Lots of designs are just solutions that lack style.

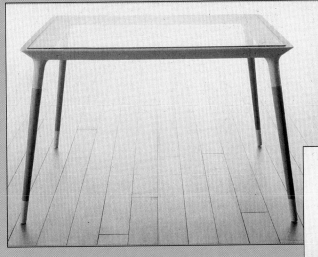

Product: Perimeter (front view and detail)
Design: Mark Goetz
Courtesy of Bernhardt Design

Product: Sofa
Design: Mark Goetz
Courtesy of Herman Miller for the Home

The Art of Observation

DESIGNER: SOPHIE DEMENGE
Title: Vice President
Firm Name: r+d design
Location: Brooklyn, New York

What do you do every day that makes you happy you chose to be a designer?
I really *look*; it makes me feel involved. It also makes me feel aware.

Product: Doily table
Designers: r+d design
Year: 2001
Description: Laser-cut and bead-blasted stainless-steel top with stainless-steel base

How did you discover product design?
By accident. My sculpture professor at San Francisco Community College offered a trial class in product design and asked if I would sign up to fill the class.

How did you decide to become a product designer?
When I discovered it was a profession. After all the fields I tried, design is the only one I still get excited about. I don't feel the time going by; nothing else matters. I love design because I think about the process without thinking about the outcome.

Who are your heroes?
My husband, Michael, for laughing with me every day, and my mother, Liza, for teaching me what's important in life.

Where do your ideas come from?

Everywhere—most of the time in the most unexpected way, which is great. It's so fun to surprise yourself. The worm bench was inspired by a trip to the biodiversity section of the Museum of Natural History in New York.

What is your most successful design?

The Somi Table, because it works in different environments— home, office—with different styles. Also it is economical and got lots of press. Its name is for my husband and myself: Sofie Demenge and Michael Ryan. We can both sit on it.

What is your favorite design?

The Doily Table, because it's the latest. Also I really like the Lubie & Pod ceramic plates; I think they are really beautiful.

Product: Somi Magazine Table
Designers: r+d design
Year: 2001
Description: Powder-coated silver base, powder-coated red-white-black top side table for phone and phonebook, laptop, or occasional table with a lamp and a place to store magazines. The light appearance belies its remarkable strength; it was tested to withstand 274 lbs (the combined weight of the designers).

Product: Worm Bench
Designers: r+d design
Year: 2001
Description: Nine feet in length, brilliant green in color, and segmented in form, the painted LDF worm bench was inspired by a field trip to the biodiversity section at the Museum of Natural History in New York. The bench marks a return to nature, playfulness, motion, and interaction reminiscent of childhood toys.

What would you design if you could?
A playground. I would get to try all sorts of things; it would be so much fun.

What are you working on now?
A baby furniture line with the babies and kids in mind, not the parents.

Product: Poulpa Stool
Designers: r+d design
Year: 2001
Description: The fiberglass Poulpa stools were inspired by forms such as banyan trees, jellyfish, and octopus. In response to today's modernism, the poulpa contradicts spare minimalism to exemplify nature's inherent beauty of proportion and form to become a functional sculpture.

Product: Three Bears' Nesting Chairs
Designers: r+d design
Year: 2001
Description: The three bears' nesting chairs communicate r+d's modernization of the childhood story and the designers' response to the space constraints of urban living. A clever contribution to the realm of nesting products, the steel chairs appear as one elegant unit until the onset of guests into the home causes smaller chairs to be withdrawn as needed.

Logic and Magic

DESIGNER: ERIC CHAN

Title: Founder
Firm Name: ECCO Design, Inc.
Location: New York City

What is product design to you?
Making everyday objects a wonderful, desirable experience for the user.

What makes you happy as a designer?
Breaking new ground and challenging new territory, from a simple toothbrush to a complex computer; bringing joy to common people; seeing my designs in people's homes and offices and in supermarkets and museums around the world. Mediating the balance between people and objects, poetry and logic, technology and nature is very fulfilling.

How did you discover product design?
By admiring beautiful objects in magazines.

What inspired you to become a product designer?
The simple desires to do beautiful things and to have other people appreciate them. My ambition is to challenge the design boundaries of everyday objects and bring them to higher ground.

Product: EC 2 Phone
Designer: Eric Chan
Client: Becker, Inc.
Year: 1990

Why did you become a product designer?
I challenge myself to utilize today's technology to create products that address harmony among nature, human beings, and society. I want to create products that make a difference in the world.

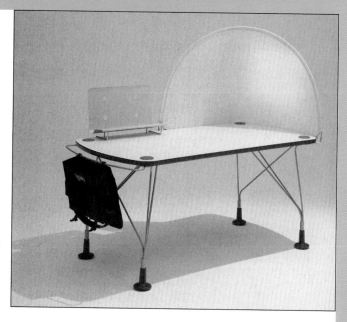

Product: Spider Table
Designers: Eric Chan, Rama Chorpash, Jeff Miller
Client: Herman Miller
Year: 2001
Photo: Ken Skalski

Product: Boston Executive Stand-up Stapler
Designers: Eric Chan, Ethan Imboden
Client: Hunt Manufacturing
Year: 2000
Photo: Ken Skalski

Who were your early influences?
Henry Moore, Charles Eames, George Nelson, Mario Bellini.

Who are your heroes? Why?
My heroes are business visionaries who integrated design intelligently into their business strategy to produce great products that are not only making a profit but also elevating the design awareness of the general public. Steve Jobs from Apple and Max DePree from Herman Miller are two great heroes who used good design to transform commercially successful products into cultural icons in our time.

What is your least favorite design?
Every design has room for improvement. We have to learn to live with mistakes and move on. Nothing is perfect. You just have to think of a better way and come up with a better solution next time.

What would you design if you could?

A truly ecological product that does not burden our ecosystem.

How do you work—in collaboration or alone?

I collaborate with a very good team of multidisciplinary talents, including a researcher, a strategist, a designer, a model maker, a CAD designer, and engineers.

Where do you get your ideas?

By observing people and the environment and by trying to understand changes in our culture and behavior.

Product: Wave Bench
Designers: Eric Chan, Jeff Miller
Client: RPI
Year: 2000
Photo: Ken Skalski

Where do you work?

Mostly in my studio, in my workshop, sometimes at home, in the shower, in bed, in the airport, on a plane, on a train—but not on the beach yet.

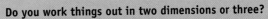

Do you work things out in two dimensions or three?

I always sketch with a pencil in 2D first, then work with a CAD designer to produce a digital model. I also make lots of mockups and models.

Do you live with your own designs?

At home I brush my teeth with my Colgate toothbrush and make calls on my EC phone. In my studio I work on my Kiva table from Herman Miller and use my Boston stand-up stapler every day.

What are you working on now?

A pen, airport seating, office furniture, a cell phone, a line of kitchen tools, and a microwave oven.

Product: Kiva Table
Designers: Eric Chan, Jeff Miller
Client: Herman Miller
Year: 2000

Color

DESIGNER: RON KEMNITZER
Title: President
Firm Name: Kemnitzer Design, Inc.
Location: Kansas City, Missouri

What is the favorite product you have designed?
This is really hard to answer because my projects are so different. In the large picture, is an automobile ice scraper any more or less important than a patient monitoring system?

How did you discover industrial design?
When I was eleven years old, growing up on a farm in Ohio, my mother gave me a copy of *Designing for People* by Henry Dreyfuss, one of the early great industrial designers who literally invented the profession. I remember my mother saying, "I think you might be interested in this, since you like both science and art so

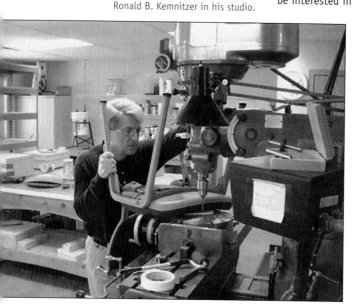

Ronald B. Kemnitzer in his studio.

much." As I read that book my future unfolded in front of me like a revelation. I've never been interested in anything else, and I have even more love for it now than ever before.

How do you work? How do you attack a design problem?
I usually begin a project with great enthusiasm and excitement but also some fear that I won't be worthy. The unknown is the root of both the enthusiasm and the fear. Projects usually start with research into what the product does and, more importantly, who uses it and how. Our office is small, so everyone contributes. We have a lot of interaction during the conceptual sketching and development stages, where many ideas feed the process and get debated and tested by many points of view. Our tools are traditional—hand

sketching—at the beginning because we believe the pencil to be a more personal, sensual, and thought-stimulating tool than computer design tools. We can also generate and test more ideas faster by hand. We use the inaccuracy of hand drawings and their misinterpretations as a creative tool in our process. One of us often interprets the sketch of another designer in a way that wasn't intended but is in fact a fresh and viable idea that can be added to the mix. We also use quick volume and form studies to fully appreciate the appropriateness of scale of design concepts and to informally test their physical efficacy. As a concept becomes more refined and developed, we introduce such computer-based design tools as three-dimensional CAD to document and test the designs. As our design efforts are user-centered, we test our designs with prototypes in realistic environments that simulate their actual use. The results of this testing help us refine the design concept to be the best possible solution.

Product: Bola
Designer: Ronald B. Kemnitzer
Client: Fixtures Furniture Co.
Year: 1998

What do you design? It seems like a varied group of products, including furniture, medical equipment, and more. Is the design process always the same?
We focus on the usability of the product to achieve an intended result with an identified user. Sometimes those criteria can be vague or not stated at all by our client. One of our tasks is to determine which criteria are most important and which are less so or totally extraneous. With continuing flux in the relative importance of criteria and user description, our design process is similar in most cases.

Do you find that designing a piece of furniture is similar to designing a medical instrument? Why?
Furniture is unique in that it is generally used by a wide variety of users who each have their own way of using it. Such broad

Product: Fit Zone
Designer: Ronald B. Kemnitzer
Client: Lee Apparel Co.
Date: 1993

Product: Kinderdoodle Preschool Desk
Client: Hopkins Manufacturing Company
Year: 2001

use patterns complicate the task by requiring anticipation of the myriad possibilities of use and misuse of the product. For instance, when you are designing a school chair, you should probably consider a maintenance worker using it as a ladder to reach a light bulb. Medical products carry the added responsibility for patient well-being, but the design might actually be more manageable because the product is likely to be used by trained personnel in a prescribed environment requiring a well-defined procedure. The increase and reduction of variables greatly affects the complexity of design.

Some designers seem to specialize, but you don't. Is that a choice or just good business? Is it just more fun?
One of the things that appealed to me so much in the Dreyfuss book was the wide variety of projects that industrial designers do. Early in my career I worked for corporations that were narrowly focused on their products, and I was bored by the repetition of the work. Since starting my own business I have by choice avoided specialization even though it might have offered more financial security at times. Everyone in our office thrives on change and uncertainty. We have found that our experiences in many areas offer continuous opportunities to transfer technologies, materials, and business practices from one category to another.

Product: QuBit Digital Image Storage Device
Client: Qu VIS, Inc.
Year: 1996

Do you have a favorite client or design experience? Something that was a surprise at the end?
I designed a chair for a client who hated the initial design

concept. I kept showing the same concept at every client review until he finally warmed up to it and said, "I always did like that one the best." It became the best-selling chair in that company's history—over a million chairs.

Do you do a lot of research? Focus groups?
Our projects are generally small in scope and don't have budgets for formal research, so we have to be efficient and creative in how we gather information. We get a lot of information through the Internet.

You seem to have a lot of fun designing. Why? Is it just in your blood?
A moment that reminded me of how lucky I am to be a designer was when my daughter introduced me to her kindergarten class by saying, "This is my dad. His job is to color." They were impressed.

Speaking of kids, have you designed stuff for kids?
The Kid's Console tote kit we did for Hopkins Manufacturing Company was designed for kids to take on car trips. The white board trays can be used for eating or coloring. The storage pockets are designed to snugly hold both crayons and fast-food French fries. There are also plenty of secret places to hide things from parents and snoopy siblings.

Can you sum up your design philosophy in one word?
No, I can't reduce my philosophy to one word—not even a few words. There are too many variables in the world. I'm just a guy who likes to color.

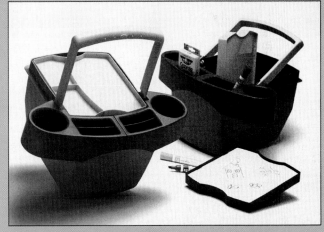

Product: Kid's Console
Client: Hopkins Manufacturing Company
Year: 1999
Photo: Don Delphia

Fit

DESIGNER: MIKE MCCOY

Title: Partner
Firm Name: McCoy & McCoy
Location: Buena Vista, Colorado

Product: Bulldog Chair
Designers: Michael McCoy, Dale Fahnstrom, and David VandenBranden, Fahnstrom/McCoy
Client: Knoll International
Description: Family of ergonomic chairs
Year: 1989

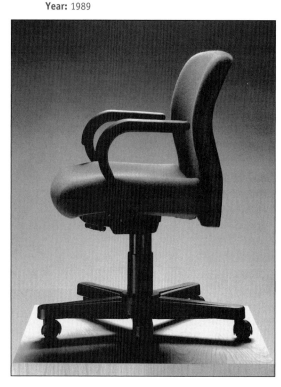

How did you discover industrial design?

In my senior year in high school I was assigned a paper on what career I would pursue. I was torn between art and engineering, but when I discovered Harold Van Doren's book on industrial design I knew immediately that this was for me.

Why did you start your own company?

After getting some experience working in a large design consulting firm I realized I liked the freedom of having my own studio and working on the projects I wanted to explore.

What was your first successful product?

The Bulldog Chair for Knoll (designed with my partner, Dale Fahnstrom) was one of my most successful projects. It has been their best-selling chair for over a decade.

You have done a lot of conceptual work. Talk about why you think this work is important. Is it meant to provoke? Startle?

I like the idea that designers can work on practical projects one day and vision projects that are meant to question or provoke the next day. I call the vision projects *design fiction* because, like science fiction, they are meant to help us see new possibilities.

You have also designed airport seating. Is designing systems different than designing products? Why?

I like systems design because you have to think about how each element affects all the other elements. It's like a chess game in which each move affects the outcome of the game.

What's your favorite project you are working on right now?

Right now I am working on a collection of furniture based on a particular system of geometry. So I am doing many pieces based on a fundamental geometric phenomena.

Has the field of industrial design changed?

The field is changing for the better in that I think the design disciplines will be working together to solve more complex projects that affect people's everyday lives.

Product: Door Chair
Designer: Michael McCoy
Year: 1981
Description: Folding chair in which the opening of the "door" creates a seat
Photo: Mike McCoy

You have won numerous awards. What was the most satisfying award and why?

The Chrysler Award for Innovation in Design (which I received with my wife, Katherine) was the most rewarding because it recognizes overall contribution to design, not just one project.

How do you hire young designers? What do you look for?

I look for a broad understanding of design and its contribution to society, not just specific skills.

How do you work? How do you attack a design problem?

1. I like to start with an understanding of how people interact with the product; that includes behavioral observation (including video ethnography).

2. The conceptual process includes quick mockups and prototypes to see if the ideas actually support people's daily routines.

3. Three-dimensional computer modeling now allows accurate communication of the designers' intent.

What goes into designing a successful product?
Understanding the real problem (and opportunity) is the fundamental starting point. From there it is matching form, technology, all aspects of human factors (physical, cognitive, and social) with the problem.

When you are designing, who finally says "this is it"?
Ideally, the designer and the client arrive at the conclusion together. If the designer has included the client in the research and conceptual process, then this has a better chance of occurring.

Do you do a lot of research? Focus groups?
We do user observations to understand how people actually interact with technology. Focus groups are usually not a good way to get insights about product breakthroughs.

Do you mock things up in your shop?
I use rough sketches and immediately start doing very rough mockups, full-scale if possible. I also try to do mockups that are robust enough so people can interact with them. I get lots of good feedback that way.

What's in the future for industrial design?
I think design is going to return to the realm of the generalist innovator away from the narrow specialist. The culture needs design to project a vision for the future that is beyond the myopic quarterly-return mentality of Wall Street.

Product: Electric Plane
Designers: Michael McCoy, Dale Fahnstrom, and David VandenBranden, Fahnstrom/McCoy
Year: 1989
Description: Home information and entertainment system comprising a giant printed circuit onto which electronic components can be placed.
Photo: Fanhstrom/McCoy

Do you have a few words of wisdom for people starting their own design business?
It is difficult to start your own studio but highly rewarding once it is up and running. You need to have a strong belief in yourself. Some of the designers I most admire have taken that entrepreneurial path, including Niels Diffrient, Bill Moggridge, and Sohrab Vossoughi.

Is it fun and exciting to see your work in use? Are you critical of it? What would you change?
One of the big rewards of design is seeing your work out in the world. Design affects people's daily lives and permeates their daily routines. I am quite critical of my own work, so I would probably change about half of it.

What is it like to own and run a small company?
The pleasure (and also the pain) of having a small company is that you have to do everything from client contact to conceptual and final design development. People who like that range of activity thrive. Specialists hate it.

What is product design?
Interpreting technology for people through physical form.

What do you do every day that makes you happy you chose to be a product designer?
I love sketching conceptual solutions to any problem I can imagine.

Can you sum up your design philosophy in one word? Why?
Fit. The designer should fit the solution to the problem.

Product: Philips Portable Audio
Designers: Michael McCoy, Dale Fahnstrom, and David VandenBranden, Fahnstrom/McCoy
Client: Philips Electronics
Year: 1987
Description: Radio/CD player that expresses its portability and audio power with cylindrical towers of molded rubber
Photo: Philips

Serendipity

DESIGNER: AYSE BIRSEL

Title: President
Firm Name: Olive 1:1, Inc.
Location: New York City

Product: Red Rocket File Cart
Designers: Ayse Birsel, Joe Stone
Creative Director: Ayse Birsel
Client: Herman Miller
Year: 2001
Photo: Bill Sharp

How did you discover industrial design?

During an afternoon tea at my parents home in Izmir. Afternoon tea is an important ritual at my parents' home, and on this particular day we were joined by a Turkish city planner who had been living in Norway. I was getting ready to enter the university exams, and we started talking about how I wanted to become an architect. The city planner asked me if I knew what industrial design was, and I told him I didn't. I really had no idea. Taking the teacup in his hand, the planner explained that there was actually a person who had designed this particular cup and who had thought about holding hot liquid in a ceramic form that needed to balance on its saucer, about how your hand would comfortably grab the cup without burning, and about how to drink from it without dripping the tea from your chin or your nose hitting the rim. He related the object constantly back to the user, the experience, and the body. Six months later, I was enrolled at the new design department of the Middle East Technical University in Ankara.

Why did you start your own company?

I started my own company because I didn't know any better. I was finishing the industrial design graduate program at Pratt Institute, New York. Bruce Hannah, who was the chair of the department and my thesis adviser, invited me to work with him on his new project for Knoll, designing a family of office accessories. I was delighted to continue to live in New York, support myself, and to have an opportunity to work with my mentor. After about a year and a half of design and development, the Orchestra Office Accessories were launched in 1990. Bruce gave me credit, and the collection to this day has both our names. It is this experience and the pride at having my name on a product that gave me the confidence and the drive to start my own company.

I didn't realize how hard it actually was going to prove to be, but I learned it soon enough as it took me another three years before I had another product on the market. That product was the Zoë Washlet for TOTO.

What was your first successful product?
The first one that got mass-manufactured.

You have also designed toilets for TOTO? What was that experience like?
That experience was as hard as it was rewarding. I never understood whether it was hard because I was a foreigner working in Japan, or because I was a woman, or because I was a designer proposing change and pushing for innovation.

I am really fond of one particular instance during the development of the Zoë Washlet for TOTO. We were in another one of our team meetings. I was proposing a snap-on, snap-off lid and seat the user could wash under the faucet or the shower. After all, a toilet that was easy to clean had to be one of our top priorities. The engineers around the table, all men, didn't see any merit to this idea. We were at a standoff until I asked them if they had ever cleaned a toilet seat in their lives. They all said no, they had not. It suddenly dawned on me that it was the women, their wives or daughters, who would take care of this chore in the house. I asked them if they'd be so kind as to try it once for my sake. The next time we met, they all came back and said yes, they now understood what I was talking about when I said easy to clean. They had cleaned their toilets over the weekend. The snap-on, snap-off seat was unanimously accepted and became one of the best features of the new design.

Product: Zoë Washlet and Prominence Toilet
Designer: Ayse Birsel
Creative Director: Ayse Birsel
Client: TOTO Ltd.
Year: 1993
Photo: Tom Vack

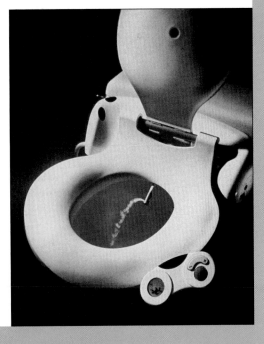

Product: Water Room
Designers: Ayse Birsel

What's your favorite project you are working on right now?
The one I know least about and learn the most from.

How do you work? How do you attack a design problem?
For any given problem, I try to observe people in their environments doing what they do—people at work, people driving cars, people at home. I try to see what is missing or awkward or stands out most. I spend a lot of time trying to see things, problems, and daily life objectively and trying to break out of current reality to see what can be fixed or made better. I open and leaf through Noguchi books when I get stuck. I sketch in my sketchbook to communicate my ideas to my team, whether it is the Olive 1:1 team or the client team. The closer I am to the product, the better my sketches. I try to listen and absorb what my clients, with all their knowledge, are telling me. I learn from them, and I try to interpret their input through my concepts. I cherish the restrictions that frame a problem. The tighter the boundaries, the more room for creativity. I like to work with intelligent people—they make for intelligent products.

When you are designing, who finally says "this is it"? The client? You?
It is the product that says, "I am it."

Is it fun and exciting to see your work in use? Are you critical of it? What would you change?
I am critical of my work when we are in the process of developing it and when there is still room for improvement. I am aware that we—the client and I—might regret some of our decisions down the line and am quite vigilant about protecting the essential points that make our idea a good one.

I have learned that one of the most effective ways to protect an idea is to write about and document it. During the development of Resolve, the Herman Miller team encouraged me to put together a concept book. Clark Malcolm, the writer on our team, and I wrote about the new rules of Resolve. There were eight basic rules, such as Be Simple, Be Economical, Be Welcoming, Make Sense, which we then explained in detail and with illustrations. This book, written while we were still in the early concept phase, became a guidebook for our development. It helped us stay on track and true to our beliefs regardless of the pressures we were constantly subjected to. It also helped arbitrate the important differences of opinion every design and development team goes through. Instead of being a battle of the egos, the discussions became one of referring to the concept book and to our main objectives. I, like the engineers, the applications designers, and the marketing group, had to check in with the original intent. If an idea was not simple enough or economical enough, it had to be rethought. In a way, the Concept Book protected Resolve from ourselves.

Can you sum up your design philosophy in one word? Why?
Serendipity. It is a one-word answer. I thought that was the neat thing about this question. Explaining *why* kills the beauty of trying to figure out a one-word answer.

Product: Resolve System
Designer: Ayse Birsel
Client: Herman Miller
Year: 1999
Photo: Herman Miller

Chapter Six

Fashion

Product design has invaded fashion in a big way. More and more fashion companies are hiring product designers to design and develop footwear, luggage, eyewear, and even clothing itself because of new materials and production methods. It's not enough any more to have an idea and sketch it. Product development is an expensive, time-consuming, and risky enterprise. Manufacturers hire product designers because they are educated to think through the product from idea through mass production.

Footwear was designed by fashion designers until companies like Nike and Puma started manufacturing high-tech shoes that everybody wanted. As sportswear became more and more specialized, running shoes weren't just running shoes anymore; the kind you bought depended on what kind of running you were doing and on what surface. One of the founders of Nike was Bill Bowerman, a track coach at the University of Oregon; he was concerned about the fit of each individual's running shoes to the point of obsession. According to the folklore surrounding his coaching technique, he was more interested in runners' feet than the rest of their body. He measured each runner's feet and made the athlete's shoes personally in his kitchen. The first Nike running shoes, with their famous waffle soles, were made in his kitchen by molding the soles in a waffle iron.

Bowerman's other concern with the design of the shoes was weight. He wanted to create the lightest shoes possible, believing his runners would have an advantage over their competition because they would lift less weight over the course of the run. This is true product development. He had a clear goal—winning—with a clear plan to achieve a winning edge.

Similarly, eyewear, although it is fashion-oriented, also was deconstructed into many areas, from sports to everyday. Again, it isn't enough to make sunglasses. Questions like where and when they are going to be worn, and by whom, all drive designers to create more and more styles of glasses. Are the sunglasses for skiing, surfboarding, fishing, baseball? You get the point. Each sport demands different qualities, not only in the lens and frame but also in the shape and even in how the glasses are held on the face. Just generating ideas is not the whole job; what's needed is observation, understanding the context in which the product will be used, and by whom. Women, men, and children all demand similar types of glasses, but each group has preferences in terms of styling, color, textures, and materials.

Fashion trends and forecasts play an important role in getting the design accepted by the market. Product designers in the fashion-conscious industries are constantly looking for new areas to design in. Understanding developments in new sports and new sports equipment gives designers an edge.

In a different way, fashion also determines what clock or vase we might buy. Fashion used to be a dirty word to designers, but more and more products are driven by fashion awareness. Staying alive in the thriving giftware business demands a complete understanding of what's hot and what's not. Staying in tune with their customers gives design manufacturers an edge.

Combining fashion with high-tech manufacturing is the future of fashion design. Designers of luggage, eyewear, shoes, vases, clocks, and so on keep one eye on fashion while pursuing fascinating explorations into what we all might be wearing and buying.

Survival

DESIGNER: LESLIE MULLER

Title: Fashion Design Director
Firm Name: Ray-Ban, A Luxottica Group Company
Location: New York City

What is your favorite product?

TYRA sunglasses is my favorite because of how popular it was. We sold hundreds of thousands of them. They are really sensual and beautiful, and to this day I see people on the street wearing them. That's a big success story.

Is TYRA also your most successful product?

The one called Anna, which the model Nikki Taylor wears in a lot of corporate ads for Liz Claiborne, is a total runaway hit. I thought it was a major snore, but I see it everywhere.

Is it fun to see your work?

I love it! What other hard material product can you design that sits on strangers' faces! I have eyewear radar; I can see my designs two blocks away.

What are you working on now?

My new favorites are for J. Lo. They are so much fresher, so much hipper, so much more innovative; it's a different audience.

Who are your design heroes?

A personal hero is my mom because she's also a designer—a graphic designer. When we were little she stayed home and designed and made furniture. I remember playing with my dolls in these little models of sofas and chairs she made. Then she'd build the wooden bodies of the full-size versions and veneer and upholster them. It was beautiful furniture, but nobody knew she made it. My mom nurtured my interest in the three-dimensional world. She exposed me at a very early age to design and showed me it had no barriers. You have more power than you think. That's why I chose industrial design as opposed to graphic design.

Do you have any mentors?

I could go on forever about Ivy Ross. She got me into the eyewear industry when she was vice president of design and development for an eyewear company called Outlook. She called me in 1993 and told me she was sending me a ticket because she needed me to design eyewear. She threw me in the deep end of the pool, and I cranked out hundreds and hundreds of drawings. She is now president of Barbie at Mattell; she's a completely innovative thinker who's got both sides of the brain firing at the same time.

What are the sources of your inspiration?

I get a lot of my ideas just walking around. And I love riding the subway! It is a great source of inspiration. I love staring at people.

What about style?

I have one foot in the world of industrial design and the other in fashion. When you are designing sunglasses, you're marrying style with something that's really functional. Each eyewear designer I know has his or her own signature and look. In eyewear, you have two seasons: a huge one for summer with 110 styles and a smaller one for fall with 35 to 40. Every six months I have to generate new styles, new ideas, but they also have to last because there's a sense of permanence with sunglasses. Styling has two meanings with eyewear. One is the actual style of the frame and the other is the trends, the look, and what works.

Product: JLO Sunglasses
Designer: Leslie Muller
Art Director: Leslie Muller
Client: JLO by Jennifer Lopez
Company: Outlook Eyewear
Description: Sunglass styles from the spring 2004 collection
Year: 2003
Photo: Gian Andrea DiStefano

Product: Materials collage
Designer: Leslie Muller
Art Director: Leslie Muller
Client: Bausch & Lomb
Description: Concept exploration in materials and colors
Year: 1998
Photo: Peter Medilek

How do you design?

It's sort of like dancing on a pinhead. The way we start is with trend services and fashion forecasting. Then I meet with designers at Liz Claiborne and now Jennifer Lopez and start sketching. I talk to the marketing people. I use materials as inspiration. I do a lot of painted techniques. I go to the factories and they try to create the pattern or colors I'm looking for. Sometimes it takes two or three years to create a color or effect. The process starts in many ways. Sometimes I start with style boards as inspiration. The more restrictions, the freer I get. If someone said to design anything I wanted, I'd probably freak out and not be able to think of a thing for a week! Restrictions keep the ideas flowing.

What about marketing?

Once the prototypes are done, we meet with the sales reps and everyone has a say. That's when I have to come up with how the frames are to be marketed: the names, groupings, graphic design, and photography. Every design now has a story. That's when I become an art director, put a spin on the visual story, and create the look of the marketing.

Is trust an issue?

You have to win a client's trust and crawl into the head of the client to find out who they are and what makes them tick. What are they going to like? I have to live and breathe who that person is. When I'm doing that, I get real quiet and don't talk to anyone; I just absorb myself in the person. The subway was invaluable working on the J. Lo line.

I think that's the beauty of being an industrial designer in fashion. Industrial designers are jacks-of-all-trades. We do product, graphics, mechanizing. You can fill a lot of voids in fashion because many people in the field can't do all that. If you can develop an intelligent way of verbalizing and presenting your ideas, you got them. I'm so glad I was educated as an industrial designer. I couldn't do this job if I hadn't been.

Frantic

DESIGNER: TIMM FENTON

Title: Design Director, New Concepts
Firm Name: Tumi, Inc.
Location: Plainfield, New Jersey

What makes you happy to be a designer?

Design forces me to utilize my talent and the profession forces me to learn new things. You can never learn everything about industrial design. That's why I love it. My title is director, but I still design, sketch, model, draft on CAD. The range of tasks makes me happy.

How did you end up designing luggage?

After graduating from RISD in the late 1980s, I did several freelance jobs—aircraft interiors with Donald Thompson, furniture with Niels Diffrient, point-of-purchase display and watches at Timex—but I really wanted to follow my passion for bicycling. After three years with Cannondale designing bike stuff and two years with Rubbermaid learning the molding processes and short development time cycles, I found Tumi. Initially I underestimated what goes into the design of luggage and soft products, but at Tumi the drive has always been toward outstandingly engineered performance-based product. Wheeled luggage, for instance, incorporates an enormous range of materials, both hard and soft, which was appropriate for me, given my background.

Product: Gemini 2000
Designer: Cannondale Corp.
Company: Cannondale
Year: 2002
Photo: Kathy Ceconi

How do you go about designing a piece of luggage?

We decided to develop the business backpack for an ad executive who had to have shoulder surgeries after lugging a 30+-pound business case on a daily basis. Our design provided improved ergonomic comfort and improved functionality and still looked smart in business environments. A lot of my inspiration comes

Product: Business Backpack
Designer: Timm Fenton
Year: 1997

from simple observation, personal use, and looking outside of the industry, which is not known as highly innovative. One reason I took the position at Tumi was that I saw an opportunity to contribute.

What was the first project you worked on?
My first project was developing a new line of product geared to the young consumer, the T-Tech group, which has soft products, backpacks, and luggage. It took a year and a half to two years to develop because new products at Tumi have to be in the 99.9 percent finished range before we'll introduce it. Sweating details—getting it right—is unparalleled compared to other places, but the process can be rewarding when you see someone using a product that works.

Do you make prototypes and test them on focus groups?
Tumi doesn't typically do focus groups only because we understand the product better than anyone. We are constant users ourselves. We frequent retail stores, travel internationally, and observe people on the streets and in airports. The typical sample process is challenging because we manufacture mostly overseas.

Product: T-Tech Backpack
Designer: Timm Fenton
Year: 1999

Typically we go through three to five samples and a couple of hard prototypes before the design intent is met. New developments usually require a couple of trips to the supplier or factory.

Tumi introduced ballistic fabrics to luggage. Is there an ongoing materials search at Tumi?

Tumi has held a leadership position for many years, but we are always wary of our competition. Lower-priced product is consistently being improved, which forces us to raise the bar. A case in point is the Fusion Z Fabric, which is basically a bomber coating applied to the exterior of the ballistic fabric that virtually doubles its abrasion resistance. It's a phenomenal enhancement you can't even see. I don't think another company in the industry invests so much in quality with respect to construction and materials.

You seem to agonize over the details. Would you say designing is in the details?

Details must always add up to a cohesive design. Without them, you don't have solid product.

How do you develop products?

We have consumer groups that place heavy focus on the fashion element. They demand design innovation while always seeking the new and different.

Product: Tumi storefront, Tokyo, Japan
Designer: David Sebens
Year: 1999
Photo: David Sebens

Do you have your own retail stores?

Yes, but, we're still very much committed to the luggage specialty shops and to sharing space with retail partners. A lot of our product's success is based on how it is presented at retail. If an interesting product is showcased properly, it usually sells, so having control of presentation allows a consistent brand message to come across.

Do you present ideas as sketches?

It depends on the complexity of the project. While we use CAD to develop the hard parts,

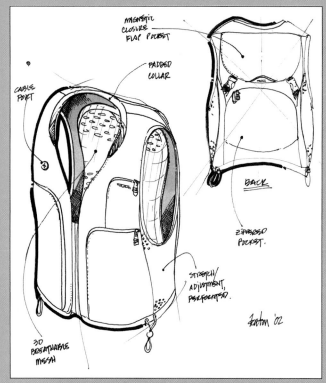

we still do a tremendous amount of hand drawing for the soft stuff. I have researched software to speed that up, but I haven't found anything faster. We try to have an actual sample made as quickly as possible. If the staff can put their hands on the item, it has more impact than images.

How do you project into the future in terms of materials?

We look beyond the obvious resources to automotive, fashion, sporting goods, even electronics. Sometimes you can get inspiration from two materials coming together on a completely unrelated product. The designer must be able to identify a potential material and envision it coming together with all the other details that will result in success. Some fabrics are beautiful but don't work well in certain shapes or with manufactured components. Some are prohibitively expensive.

Product: Travel Vest
Designer: Timm Fenton
Year: 2002
Photo: DZINE Inc.

Designing luggage is still a challenge. You haven't done the ultimate bag?

I think it's because Tumi sets such high standards and has a we-can-do-better attitude. The fascination I have with luggage is the mix of hard and soft goods harmonizing with the details. What we are working on now is how to create products that are softer but still hold shape and that are lighter, more functional, and comfortable to travel with. T-Tech began that process, but there is a long way to go.

Can you sum up your design philosophy in one word?

Frantic. Once you identify the design opportunity, it becomes a frantic process to get it completed and to market quickly.

There's a lot of talk about luggage and other wearable things incorporating electronics. Do you see this happening?

Absolutely! It's not only talk, it's happening now. Generations have been brought up on electronics. As designers, it's our responsibility to keep up with the frantic pace of change.

Product: Tumi Superlight Collection
Designer: Timm Fenton
Year: 2002

Starting Up

DESIGNERS: GIOVANNI PELLONE
BRIDGET MEANS

Title: Partners
Firm Name: Benza, Inc.
Location: Brooklyn, New York

Who is your audience?
Our products address a multicultural audience of upwardly mobile urban professionals of both sexes between twenty and forty-five. They are mostly college-educated, have an interest in the arts, and are often employed in creative fields.

How did Benza start?
We were tired of servicing clients and wanted to do our own stuff. Giovanni had designed a cardboard trash can as a student research project, so we wanted to see if we could sell it. We took a booth at the International Gift Fair in New York City and quickly found out nobody would order from a company making just one product. We had to make other products to sell the trash can.

How do you choose products to design?
We don't care if people like our products as long as we like them. We also want to be able to afford our own products.

How do you work?
We naïvely started designing for ourselves—a very selfish process—but it's much more pleasurable than designing for someone else.

  Bridget is a trained graphic designer and Giovanni is a trained industrial designer, which provides a good balance. We do all the design, engineering, manufacturing, marketing, and sales of our products. We design the products, then outsource either the entire product or the parts. We do the quality control and assembly in-house. Basically, we are a design studio that promotes what we design.

Product: Zago folding trash cans
Designers: Giovanni Pellone,
Bridget Means
Year: 1996
Photo: Giovanni Pellone

Product: Aracnolamp
Designers: Giovanni Pellone
Year: 2001
Photo: Giovanni Pellone

Product: Mutant Vase
Designer: Giovanni Pellone
Year: 1998
Photo: Giovanni Pellone

Is this a new approach to a design studio?
We reversed the roles by having manufacturers work for us.

How do you manufacture the products?
We do just-in-time manufacturing, and we're able to assemble and ship up to 1,000 products a day. Products share parts; all the clocks use the same mechanism and hands. That cuts down on inventory and allows flexibility.

What is the range of products Benza makes?
There are five collections, including clocks, mouse pads, and tabletop items, which add up to about 100 products. We stay within a certain size and price range to avoid manufacturing and distribution problems.

Your products are whimsical and humble at the same time. Is this intentional?
Making expensive stuff was never our goal. We want people to see the humor and silliness in our products. They won't save your life physically, but they might make you smile.

Where did the name Benza come from?
Bridget came up with "Design is fuel for our products," and the Italian slang word for gasoline is *benza*. It means "toilet seat" in Japan, which in some weird way works there. In Tibet, *benza* means "thunderbolt." So the name travels the world pretty well.

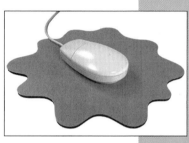

Product: Squiggle mousepad
Designers: Giovanni Pellone, Bridget Means
Year: 1997
Photo: Giovanni Pellone

Product: Peacock hanging placemats and coasters
Designer: Giovanni Pellone
Year: 1999
Photo: Giovanni Pellone

Who buys your products?

We sell directly to museum stores and high-end design stores. Our website is our most important promotional tool to retail customers. Our image is very, very important, and we look for people who will protect it. We sell in Europe, but there's more competition from small design manufacturers there.

Do you do trade shows?

Trade shows provide a focused group of buyers, so they're our most successful sales activity.

Product: Flowerfish clock
Designers: Giovanni Pellone, Bridget Means
Year: 2002
Photo: Giovanni Pellone

Product: Boing dish
Designer: Giovanni Pellone
Year: 1998
Photo: Giovanni Pellone

Product: Sticky clock
Designers: Giovanni Pellone, Bridget Means
Year: 2000
Photo: Giovanni Pellone

New!

DESIGNER: VICTORIA BEVAN

Title: Design Director, Merchandising & Advanced
Selling Systems, Worldwide
Firm Name: Clinique
Location: New York City

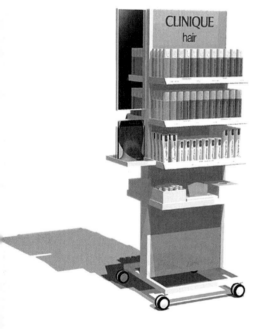

Product: Hair Care Kiosk rendering
Designers: Victoria Bevan,
Scott Blair
Creative Director: Scott Blair
Year: 2000

How did you discover industrial design?
I was a first-year architecture student, but I was not enjoying the theoretical part of the course work. I still love architecture, but switching to industrial design gave me what I needed: realistic creativity with the option to infuse as much or as little conceptualization as I wanted.

How do you work? How do you attack a design problem?
At Clinique, I work in a more structured manner than I might if left to my own devices. Once the marketing department has decided they have a merchandising need and the budget to fund it, they send us paperwork describing what they want. My first step is to get as much information as I can. The information makes me a better designer. I ask what the product does, why they are launching it now, what the visual for the launch is, and what the promotional copy will be. For the smaller projects, like tester units, the next step is to gather the products, since in the end we are creating the best display for the products, not the best display on its own merit. I start thinking about possible materials, and we start by sketching by hand, rough concepts— sometimes alone, sometimes as a group. Next, we move on to a rough computer layout just to check our scale.

We go through at least two levels of approval within the creative department, which narrows our candidates to two or three, and the process is collaborative. At this stage, we usually also get a vendor involved for a pricing study, because if we can't make something within budget, it won't get made.

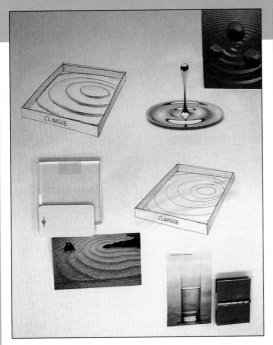

Product: Water Therapy Tester Unit
Designers: Victoria Bevan,
Sang Yun Shin, Cheryl Peyton
Creative Director: Jane Mauksch
Year: 2003

Next is model time. Depending on the complexity and the materials, we do a rough mockup in-house. Someone on my staff does the model studies. Foamcore and plexi sheets are our preferred materials because we do not have a shop, just a cutting station.

The marketing department usually sees ideas in model form only. Then, one gets approved based on a multitude of factors.

Designing products must be a challenge, given the design constraints. How do you maintain a consistent company image?

We consistently use specified materials and colors—that helps a lot. Making the whole look good versus creating individuality for product lines is an ongoing battle between creative and marketing. We are trying to communicate the company philosophy to the consumer through all aspects of what they see in store, from the counter to the product to the poster and the consultant.

Is there a product you have designed that makes you happy?

What makes me happy is when I design something that fulfills all of the requirements, passes the grueling approval process, and

Product: Gentle Light Makeup and Powder Product Launch Tester
Designers: Victoria Bevan, Denise Delong
Creative Director: Scott Blair
Year: 2001

Product: Tokyo Color Deck
Prototype
Designers: Victoria Bevan, Scott
Blair, Sojiro Inoue
Creative Director: Scott Blair
Year: 2000

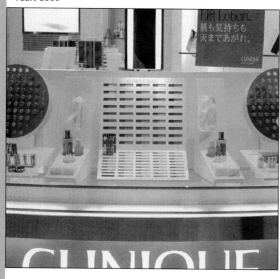

still manages to be a design I am proud of. Different projects are satisfying for different reasons. Sometimes the finished piece is something I am proud of, and sometimes it is the actual process of doing the project.

Where do you get your ideas?
Sometimes the product packaging, sometimes the technology of the product, sometimes the advertising concept tie-in. Mostly, ideas come by just talking about it, piecing together mood boards.

When you are designing, who finally says "this is it"? The client? You?
The final decision is made by the client, and in my case the client is almost always the internal Clinique marketing group. We have a lot of discussions, though, and I always stand up for ideas I feel strongly about.

Do you have a favorite client or design experience?
Certainly some clients are easier to work with than others. The best clients are those who understand that the design of an object is as important as the technology or the marketing of that object.

Is designing fun?
Absolutely. It never ends. Your next design can always be better than the last, and it should be.

What's in the future for industrial design?
We need to be doing more with less. Hopefully we can reduce the production of future landfill.

Do you have a few words of wisdom for people starting out in the design business?
Do anything—for free, if you must—but make sure you do it in a place or industry in which you can see yourself five years from now. If you want to be a toy designer, don't settle for anything less.

Is it fun and exciting to see your work in use? Are you critical of it? What would you change?
I love to see finished projects in the stores, but most of the time, there are things I would change. Because most of our ideas go through many stages and end up being collaborations, most finished pieces seem unfamiliar to me in a personal way.

What is product design?
The infusion of style, experience, and functionality into everyone's life, every day.

Why did you become a designer?
I was excited by the broad possibilities. You can design tractors or toothbrushes and everything in between. It's not really possible to get bored.

Where do you get your ideas?
Everywhere. Nature, machines, art.

How do you work? In collaboration? Alone?
Mostly I work alone first, then move to a group for opinions and input. Sometimes we start as a team, brainstorming, sketching, and talking all together in the same room at the same time.

Is there a design that never got made?
Really, none of them get made—at least not exactly in the way I first see them.

Can you sum up your design philosophy in one word? Why?
New. If it isn't new, then why bother? I have no interest in restyling a cell phone casing. It's much more interesting to think about a new way to communicate.

Product: Clinique Service Center
Designers: Victoria Bevan, Denise Delong, Scott Blair
Creative Director: Scott Blair
Year: 1999

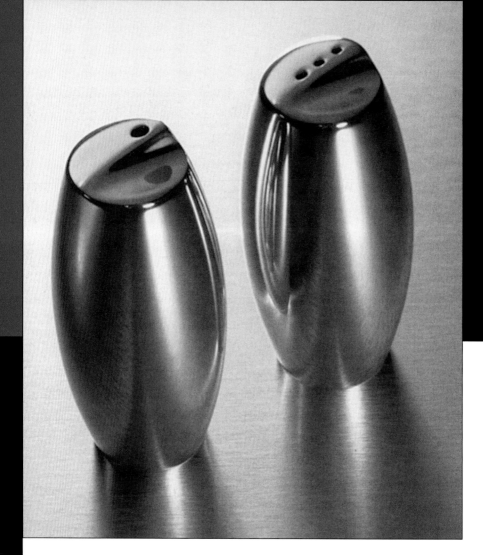

Chapter Seven

Tabletop: Putting Food on the Table

Every time you eat, a designer had something to do with how the food was served, presented, packaged, or cooked. Tabletop is a broad area inhabited by product designers. From the plate on which the food is served to the utensils it is eaten with to the look of the food itself, designers were involved. Tiffany and Target employ industrial designers to design their products. The markets may vary but the problem is the same—designing products that are beautiful and functional. Cups, mugs, glasses, dishes, serving plates, bowls, knives, forks, spoons, vases, napkins, pitchers—everything that's needed to set a table is designed. And it's designed for different environments, from casual to formal from picnics to takeout.

The kind of food—Mexican, Japanese, home-grilled burgers—influences the look of the table. Designers create tableware for specific restaurants, from Le Cirque to Joe's Stone Crab. Every situation influences the designer's decisions. Materials play a huge role in what diners expect. Tabletop designers work with plastic, fine china, stainless steel, sterling silver, wood—just about every material is used in the creation of the products we use to entertain.

Russel and Mary Wright, in the 1940s and 1950s, designed tabletop products that changed how we eat, drink, and entertain at home, helping create a new American lifestyle. Until the 1950s, entertaining at home meant Sunday dinner. As the American middle class grew, entertaining became less formal, with guests standing around talking, eating, and drinking. This was a huge departure, and hosts needed new products to support this new style. The Wrights used the picnic as their prototype for informal entertainment. Guests were expected to serve themselves from a buffet, sometimes even from pots on the stove. Entertaining became a cooperative effort; guests not only served themselves but also helped clean up afterwards. We take this type of entertaining for granted now, but the Wrights helped create it. Their book, *Easier Living* (1950), not only explained how to go about doing it but also helped market the products they designed. Many Wright-designed products are sought-after collectibles. More recently we have looked to Martha Stewart and K-Mart to guide us to gracious living.

The tabletop area of industrial design is also growing to address concerns with the independence of people at the extremes of age—the elderly and the very young. These areas of design didn't exist a few years ago, but just go to Buy Buy Baby and see all the eating utensils for babies and youngsters. Older people whose continued independence can be facilitated by good design are demanding that their concerns be addressed by designers, and so more and more such products are becoming available for them.

The markets for tabletop are endless. Airlines commission industrial designers to design and develop their food service tableware. Just think resorts, cruise ships, hotels, camping, and there's a whole bunch more industries that want to distinguish themselves from the competition for our free time. Chain restaurants design their own tableware. The next time you eat at Applebee's or Olive Garden, look at the tableware; it was specifically designed for them.

As branding becomes more and more the norm, designers will be commissioned to help brand everything a company uses, not just what it sells. Tabletop design is a huge area of product design, as varied as any of the other industrial design specialties, but an area where the product designer gets to use just about every kind of material, from the mundane to the precious. Few other areas can say that.

Nature

DESIGNER: LINDA CELENTANO

Title: Founder
Firm Name: Linda Celentano, Inc.
Location: Waldwick, New Jersey

How did you discover industrial design?
In first grade, when I made my first abacus out of Cheerios.

How do you work? How do you attack a design problem?
I begin designing three-dimensionally. That's where I get my best ideas. Sometimes I work in miniature. My three-dimensional designs are often shown to buyers or individuals from major magazine publications. These aren't prototypes but really good concept sketches.

How did you discover tabletop design?
When I first saw the Rosenthal showroom as a student.

When you are designing, who finally says "this is it"? The client? You?
Myself and my client.

Do you do a lot of research? Focus groups?
My clients do the focus groups. I am too emotional to run a focus group. It feels like my life is on the line. I prefer to concentrate on designing and manufacturing.

What's in your future? What do you want to design?
Tabletop will always be my favorite area. Sculpting may be on the horizon as well.

Who are your clients?
Nambé and Rosenthal are my main clients. My most recent work is the crystal bowls I designed for Rosenthal and the salad servers I

Product: Salad Servers
Designer: Linda Celentano
Client: Nambé
Year: 2002

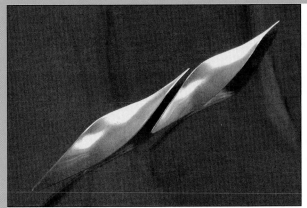

Spiral Letter Opener and Vases by Linda Celentano and Lisa Smith for Celentano and Nambé

designed for Nambé. I feel I discovered new ideas here. I always think of Rowena Reed Kostellow, who referred to designing as a visual laboratory.

Is it fun and exciting to see your work in use? Are you critical of it?
I'm always astonished to see my designs in someone's living room. Once it is designed and out there, I'm usually no longer critical of it. I've analyzed my work so much while designing it that I no longer need to improve it.

What is product design?
Good design is something you want to live with.

Why did you become a designer?
I liked making beautiful things.

What were your early influences?
Discovering nature and studying with Rowena Reed Kostellow, Dr. William Fogler, and Gerald Gulotta.

What is your most successful design? What makes it successful?
My Spiral Vases for Nambé. I just like looking at them.

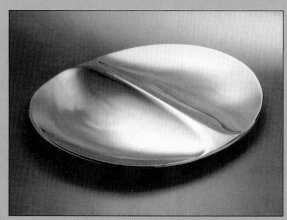

Symphony Server
by Linda Celentano

Spiral platter by Linda Celentano
for Nambé

What is your least favorite design?
A pair of eyeglasses I designed. It won a lot of awards,
but they are not my favorite because they are not organic
in nature. They are static relationships, but in retrospect
they really should have been organic.

How do you work? In collaboration? Alone?
Alone.

Do you have a favorite designer?
Eva Zeisel.

**Can you sum up your design philosophy in one word?
Why?**
Nature. Marc Chagall said it best: I know my work is
successful when it doesn't clash with nature.

Product: Salad Servers
Designers: Linda Celentano, Tucker Viemeister,
Annie Breckenfeld, Brent Marke
Company: Smart Design
Client: Copco
Year: 1986
Photo: Thomas Dair

Tea Pod by Linda Celentano for Nambé

Passion!

DESIGNER: LISA SMITH

Title: President
Firm Name: Smithereens
Location: New York City

How do you work? How do you attack a design problem?

I usually start with a sketch in my ever-present sketchbook, which is like a diary of ideas. I quickly move to three-dimensional study sketches and go back and forth between 2D and 3D as I develop an idea and a form.

Designing furniture must be a challenge, given the high volumes and design constraints. What goes into designing a successful piece of furniture?

My most successful piece of furniture is still selling better than ever after ten years. What makes it successful? When I conceived it, I challenged myself to make a stacking chair more beautiful. Most stacking chairs are static in appearance, while the form of my chair is more dynamic. I also employed efficient wood technology. Steam-bending the wood allowed for fewer joints, so the chair could be more efficiently and economically manufactured.

When you are designing, who finally says "this is it"? The client? You?

I like to be the final OK, and my clients like that too. That's why they hire me. We value one another's judgment.

Product: Chorus Stacking Chair by Gunlocke
Designer: Lisa Smith
Client: Gunlocke Company
Date: 1992

Product: Nambé Spiral Series
Designers: Lisa Smith,
Linda Celentano
Client: Nambé Mills
Years: 1996–2000

Do you do a lot of research? Focus groups?

This depends entirely on the project. A good example of a current project that requires a lot of research and will continue to is a new material I am using for cookware. We are doing finite element analysis, heat transfer analysis, material testing, composition analysis weight testing, and on and on before the cookware goes to market. Cookware is a complex product that requires a considerable amount of research and development.

When you are designing, how do you work? Do you mock things up in your shop?

I have a pretty good shop for working three-dimensionally. I just purchased a rapid prototyping tool, which I am having fun with. But I will always mock things up from cardboard, wood, plastic, and the like.

You seem to have a lot of fun designing. Why?

I have a passion for finding solutions and simple, elegant forms.

What' s in your future? What do you want to design?

I am fascinated with lighting. I want to design beautiful lighting that uses energy-efficient solutions. I think there is a real need for it.

Do you have a few words of wisdom for people starting their own design business?
Work passionately.

Who are your clients?
Steelcase, Haworth, HON Industries, Gunlocke, Davis Furniture, Nambé Mills, Rosenthal, Levenger, Fasem, Bonacina, and others. I design with these guidelines: (1) an object must be beautiful, (2) it should fill our lives with ease and accessibility, not complexity, (3) and the materials and manufacturing process should be well chosen, economical, and not wasteful.

What do you do every day that makes you happy you chose to be a product designer?
I invent in my sketchbook and then I go into the studio and build it. If it's a sunny day, I am in heaven.

Why did you become a designer?
I think I do it well.

What is your favorite design?
I love them all.

What is your least favorite design?
I don't remember.

Where do you get your ideas?
My ideas come from my needs. I am always thinking about how I can improve my own existence.

Do you work things out two- or three-dimensionally?
Observation and research contribute importantly to developing a

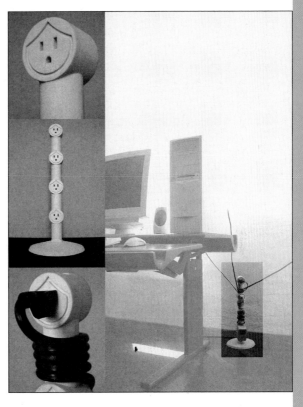

Product: Trudy Cable Management
Designers: Lisa Smith, Marit Meisler
Year: 2003

Product: Zebra
Designers: Lisa Smith, Marit Meisler
Client: World Wildlife Foundation
Year: 2002
Photo: Marit Meisler

product idea, but my design process naturally begins with a pencil sketch. Then I am quick to move to three-dimensional sketch models. I build an idea three-dimensionally so I can analyze the form as I'm designing and developing it.

What was your most recent purchase?
The OXO teakettle. It looks great on my stove and, most of all, I like picking it up and pouring from it. It makes the process of pouring boiling water safer.

What are you working on now?
Lighting, children's furniture, a folding chair, cookware, and dinnerware. I hope some of these projects make it to market in this economy.

Can you sum up your design philosophy in one word?
Passion. You gotta have it.

"Where Do You Get Your Ideas?"

I try to find ideas from something seemingly unrelated and extrapolate its essence to arrive at new and fresh ideas. That's a good way to avoid sophomoric design statements.
—Trevor Combs, Super Innovative Concepts, Inc.

Usually great ideas come from other categories, meaning if you are developing a product for the hardware industry you might use an idea from a housewares project you just completed.
—Paul Metaxatos, Proteus Design

From my mistakes. Or better put, discoveries are my best ideas.
—Linda Celentano, Linda Celentano, Inc.

Everywhere. Stuff I see, needs I find, combinations of things, growing, traveling, watching, doing, making, etc.
—Tucker Viemeister, Springtime-USA

From interacting with other people about a project. They usually say or do something that stimulates a solution.
—Peter Bressler, Bresslergroup, Inc.

I love to walk. I make a conscious effort to remain aware of the world around me in an energized way. Inspiration can sneak in from the oddest places you'll miss if your mind isn't open and ready to take it in. Good magazines are a source of inspiration and a knowledge base for what's out there, what's not, and opportunities I can capitalize on as a designer. I also read the *Wall Street Journal* every day cover to cover. Design is a business, and what designers do is very much a part of the world of dollars and cents. I need to understand that for the way it directly impacts my work.
—Joel Delman, Product Development Technologies

I enjoy walking through department and specialty stores to see what's around. I go to trade shows like the International Housewares Show or the Tabletop Show to see what's going on in new products. It's important to be aware of what other people are doing and which companies pay serious attention to design.
—George Schmidt, George Schmidt, Inc.

I get many ideas from carefully observing the world. Ideas are a bit like radio waves; they're all around us. The more I'm able to contemplate and focus on a given problem, the clearer the solution becomes.
—Mario Turchi, ION Design

Just look at the world; the ideas are right in front of you. Just watch people use things and then create things for their functional aspects. The aesthetic attributes are usually in nature.
—Davin Stowell, Smart Design LLC

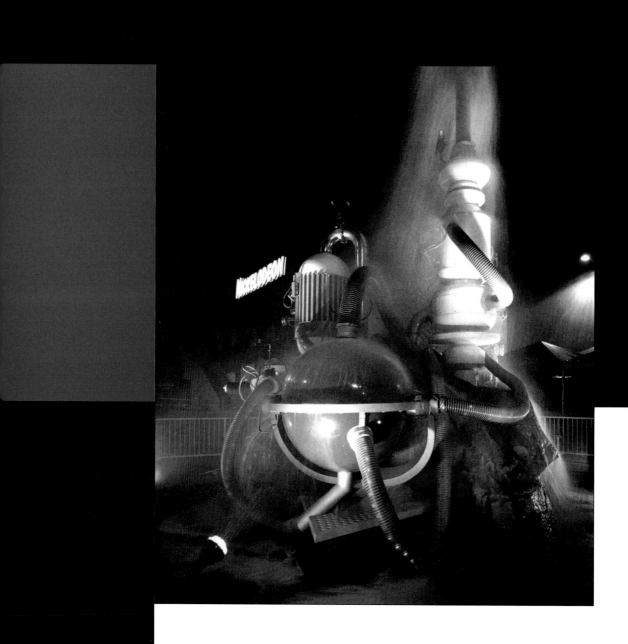

Chapter Eight

Exhibit Design

Exhibit design includes trade shows, permanent museum installations, and temporary installations. Its essence is designing experiences that inform and educate. The message is the most important part of exhibit design; conveying to the audience complex ideas and concepts is the challenge. Exhibit designers are edutainers; they must both entertain and educate at the same time. (Sometimes entertainment is the only goal; the Nickelodeon Slime machine is pure entertainment, sliming the audience in a splash of green while belching.)

Exhibit designers work with every sense. They want us to feel, see, hear, taste, and smell whatever experience they are trying to convey. Immersion in the experience is their goal. If we are descending into the abyss of the ocean, we should experience it in every way we can, from the sound to the way light filters through the water. Exhibit designers usually work with curators who gather the information and items to be displayed and create a script of the text and images that make up the exhibit. The designer usually starts with this script, which precisely details the objects, experiences, and text to be included in the exhibit. Most exhibits now are produced simultaneously with an accompanying book; this also helps the designer to understand the material.

Once the script is understood and digested, the designer will make proposals as to what form the exhibit might take. These are usually quick sketches or models that express the kinds of experiences the audience will have. Once a direction is chosen, the designer begins to expand on these ideas and develop more elaborate proposals. Exhibit design is storytelling in three dimensions. The structure, form, color, lighting, and text all must work together creating a complex experience that allows each viewer to take away something different.

Unlike most designs, it is difficult to define accurately who will visit a given exhibit, so exhibit designers must create an experience that appeals to everyone, from the eight-year-old to his grandmother and everyone in between. Designers in this area have embraced universal design, using every means at their disposal to improve access for all, including talking rails, Braille signage, and tape-recorded exhibition tours. Exhibition designers are constantly finding new ways to communicate ideas to a broad audience.

Exhibits range in scale from simple kiosks that give directions or make a single point to major product introductions that cover entire exhibit halls and convention centers. Automobile companies introduce their new lines at major automobile shows, where experimental designs are tested on the public to see what they like and dislike. Electronics companies introduce new products and new concepts in communication to the public and their dealers at giant shows in Las Vegas. Exhibit designers get the inside track on all this new stuff. And they get to create environments both fantastic and realistic, sometimes in the same space. Whether the product is automobiles, electronics, dinosaurs, chemicals, rugs, furniture, or books, exhibit designers are involved in creating the displays that help visitors learn what's new, exciting, and intriguing. Exhibit design is much like set design in the theater. It's show time! Telling a good story and having the audience get it is the goal of every exhibit designer.

Be of Service

DESIGNER: LOUIS NELSON

Title: President and Director of Design
Firm Name: Louis Nelson Associates, Inc.
Location: New York City

What makes you happy when you come to work?
I'm happy that the office is growing in the quality of the projects we are working on. And I'm happy because I see a great deal of opportunity, largely because of the events of 9/11, for how design can be of service to the country and the people of New York City. I've always looked at how to be helpful. I'm really in a service business.

Product: No Nonsense packaging
Designer: Louis Nelson
Client: Kayser Roth
Year: 1973
Description: The market strategy naming, packaging, and merchandising of No Nonsense Panty Hose changed the aisles of supermarkets, made the color orange belong to this singular product, and for the first time offered inexpensive sheer hosiery to a fashion-conscious American public.
Photo: Melabee Miller

You've designed in all sorts of scales, from packaging to monuments to large environments. Do you use the same design process every time?
The process is always the same. When my staff or I don't follow the process, we run into problems. The first thing I do is find out what a problem is all about. Then I figure out the ideas to solve it. Once we pick the idea, we develop it. Then it's easy. The only things that get in the way are distribution problems, cost issues, details. Everything is in the concept. You can't do a concept unless you have some perception of the real needs or the perceived needs. But it has got to be more than just fulfilling some sort of immediate need or satisfaction, though there's nothing wrong with that. Years ago, when we designed pantyhose packaging, we came up with a package and a name that didn't demean women. All the packaging up to that time was extraordinarily demeaning. So No Nonsense provided a good product at a good price that was packaged in a direct way.

Years after designing No Nonsense pantyhose, you won a commission to take part in the design of the Korean War Memorial. Did you bring that same humanistic attitude to the Korean War Memorial?

Yes, but it also involved bringing an understanding to those who know nothing about the Korean War. The memorial had to coexist with other prominent memorials: the Lincoln Memorial, the Vietnam War Memorial, and the Washington Monument. They wanted a mural on a wall, but the memorial would be near one of the most successful walls ever built: the Vietnam Wall with all the names. How do you do something distinctive and also serve the purpose of coexistence? I searched in my own history to

Product: Korean War Veterans Memorial
Designer: Louis Nelson
Client: American Battle Monuments Commission
Year: 1995
Description: This powerful 164-foot-long mural, created to be "a memorial portrait etched on the nation's heart . . . a touchstone to history," is composed of over 2,000 photographed portraits of American soldiers, men and women of the Army, Navy, Air Force, and Marines. Etched on Academy Black granite panels, it stands on the Mall in Washington, D.C.
Photo: Jeff Goldberg

understand the effect the Korean War had on me. I think it's impossible to be detached as a designer. You have to be a part of your solution for any design.

I did a lot of reading about the war. It was far bloodier than Vietnam; we lost 54,000 in three years. I researched images of war from Mathew Brady's time during the Civil War to David Douglas Duncan, who took moving photographs of a Marine battalion in Korea. There is one common thread, and that's the look in people's eyes. That's what I wanted to put on the wall. At the same time I'm thinking traditional form, which is a sculpture of a great person, like at the Lincoln Memorial. The Vietnam War Memorial is essentially a restatement, masterfully done by Maya Lin, of another traditional form of monument: putting messages on walls. The only other way people honor service is by putting a portrait of their loved one on their mantel. So we developed a mural of portraits of real people who served in Korea, and it became the nation's mantel. The images are etched into a reflective surface so you can see yourself, and you become part of the past and part of the future.

Product: AirTrain station platform showing clear directional sign system suspended with minimal supports.
Designer: Staff of Louis Nelson Associates
Creative Director: Louis Nelson
Client: Port Authority of New York and New Jersey
Year: 2003
Photo: Louis Nelson Associates

What's your favorite product?

My favorite is always the thing I'm working on now. Right now I'm working on the AirTrain, a new public transit system linking Kennedy Airport to Manhattan.

Talk a little more about the AirTrain.

AirTrain is the largest mass transit program in the last half century, although it's been on the books since the late 1950s. People will be able to board a Long Island Railroad train at the new Penn Station in Manhattan and get off at the new Jamaica Station, which will be completed in 2003, and then walk probably 300 feet to the new AirTrain for a short ride to Kennedy Airport, where it will make a loop of all the terminals. The time from Penn Station to Kennedy is 38 minutes, and it will cost $11. You can check your baggage at Penn Station and pick it up at your destination.

What are your duties?

We're responsible for the train technology; it's a light rail system developed by Bombardier that's been around for a while. We're not using magnetic levitation, but

AirTrain

RAIL LINK

A
HOWARD BEACH

STATION

B
LEFFERTS BLVD

TERMINAL

4

TERMINAL

5/6

Product: AirTrain station identity system and sign face detail showing typography and symbol application.
Designer: Staff of Louis Nelson Associates
Creative Director: Louis Nelson
Client: Port Authority of New York and New Jersey
Year: 2003
Photo: Louis Nelson Associates

the quality of the ride will be reliably good; the nature of the architecture is very good. We initially started working with the Port Authority architectural team on all the information systems. As the team leader, I had to pull five disparate systems together because they all come together at Jamaica Station. We're also responsible for all the signage and all the street furniture—train platform portals, places of entrance, and things like that. Our task is to make sure weary travelers are able to find their way to New York without any problem.

What else?

Everyone uses brightly colored skis these days. My team is responsible for getting Head Ski into multicolored ski technology.

How did that happen?

In the 1970s everyone was doing black skis built around various technologies for performance. But a revolution was happening at that time, and everyone wanted to be different. New materials were coming out. There was a fashion revolution. We changed to a

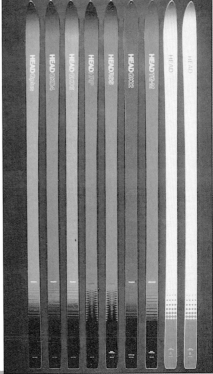

Product: Head Skis
Designer: Louis Nelson
Creative Director: Louis Nelson
Client: Head
Year: 1970
Description: Louis Nelson revolutionized the ski industry with the use of color, moving this successful line of skis beyond the typical black standard. The spectrum of color designates a skill level and relates to the psychological mindset of the skier, from beginner to expert.
Photo: Melabee Miller

spectrum of colors so the whole line of Head Skis would stand out. The subtext to that story is that the marketing forecast for the hottest color was purple. But the engineering team said, "Men don't buy purple." By the time the skis got to market, the hottest-selling ski was purple. So men buy purple.

Product: DAG Hammarskjold Medal
Designer: Louis Nelson
Creative Director: Louis Nelson
Company: Louis Nelson Associates, Inc.
Client: United Nations
Year: 1998
Description: This simple crystal, designed to be held in the palm of a widow, a mother, a father, commemorates the fragility, purity, and strength of those men and women, military and civilian, from all over the world who have lost their lives while serving with the United Nations Peacekeeping Operations. Its nontraditional shape emphasizes the bestowment of the award as a posthumous benediction, not to be worn but to be displayed in a family home.
Photo: Skalski

Nutrition Facts

Serving Size 7 Wafers (29g)
Servings Per Container About 8

Amount Per Serving

Calories 120   Calories from Fat 20

	% Daily Value*
Total Fat 3g	**4%**
Saturated Fat 0.5g	**3%**
Polyunsaturated Fat 0g	
Monounsaturated Fat 1g	
Cholesterol 0mg	**0%**
Sodium 160mg	**6%**
Total Carbohydrate 22g	**7%**
Dietary Fiber 4g	**15%**
Sugars 0g	
Protein 3g	

Vitamin A 0%	•	Vitamin C 0%
Calcium 0%	•	Iron 8%

* Percent Daily Values are based on a 2,000 calorie diet. Your daily values may be higher or lower depending on your calorie needs:

	Calories:	2,000	2,500
Total Fat	Less than	65g	80g
Sat Fat	Less than	20g	25g
Cholesterol	Less than	300mg	300mg
Sodium	Less than	2,400mg	2,400mg
Total Carbohydrate		300g	375g
Dietary Fiber		25g	30g

Product: FDA Nutrition Label
Designer: Louis Nelson
Creative Director: Louis Nelson
Company: Robert P. Gersin Associates
Client: FDA
Year: 1979
Description: Louis Nelson initiated the research and design effort to develop and implement nutritional labels for the FDA. This label is the standard on the billions of packaged food goods referred to by the American public each day, giving them information to make healthful choices.

Context

DESIGNER: KATE HIXON

Title: President
Firm Name: Hixon Design Consultants, Inc.
Location: New York City

How do you create a space in a space?

Through contrast and organization. In the case of the FAO Schwarz doll department, we achieved this by creating a visual identity separate from the store itself. We used unique display fixtures, graphics, and flooring to distinguish yet unify the individual product lines within the space. The result is a visually branded environment, where the forms and finishes become the interior architecture over that of the box.

We were then asked to do their Los Angeles flagship store. Although the store was smaller than most and full of columns, it was expected to display the same amount of product as larger stores. By the time we laid out the space with shelving and floor displays, only the ceiling was left for any special design treatment to give the space character.

So where a column hit the ceiling, we created color lighting zones to differentiate between departments. This also became a way of animating the plain white box without taking any floor space. In addition to the interior architecture and fixtures, we designed the feature clock tower and a giant mechanical toy soldier that sits over the outside entrance tipping his hat and twitching his mustache.

Product: FAO Shwartz
Designers: Hixon Design Consultants
Creative Director: David Niggli
Client: FAO Shwartz
Year: 2001

Was it a thrill to design a toy store?

It was fun, and certainly a break from our core corporate business—but thrill? We get a thrill out of making things—refining the design as we go. This process was different for us because we didn't build it. The real estate development people ran the project. We did a model, finish boards, and control drawings, after which we handed it over for the client to build. We had very little quality control.

Product: Grand Central Partnership
Designers: Hixon Design Consultants
Creative Director: Kate Hixon
Client: Jones Lang LaSalle
Year: 1999

Do you enter design competitions?

Typically not. However, the project for the seasonal marketplace at Grand Central's Vanderbilt Hall was the result of a competition. We wanted to create retail fixtures or booths that would complement the architectural character of the space. We had to start with planning the space for function, traffic flow, and financial viability. It turned into a grid of 8- by 10-foot booths. So we did a massing model to see how we could minimize this effect. We proportioned the height of the units and angled the sides to complement the ceiling height and the chandeliers in the space. The wall panels are made up of translucent panels with etched graphics to diffuse seasonal colored lighting. Ribbonlike signs further animate the space with color and add a sense of celebration.

What is your most successful project?

The before and after shots of the Pfizer lobby renovation convince me that it was a successful project—but the real success is in the continued relationship that has grown from that initial project. We continue to evolve their corporate headquarters toward a unified vision, one project at a time.

What would you like to design if you could?
Absolutely anything, but my favorite expression is always in the use of space as an abstract design medium—so, I guess, interior and exterior architecture.

How did the Ernst & Young project come about?
It was a result of an unsuccessful project. But they liked our ideas well enough to keep us involved. Ernst & Young's ad campaign has a simple minimalist look—black and white graphic icons with catchy phrases. We were asked to transform these advertisements into window displays for their new headquarters in Times Square. Our challenge was to meld the sophisticated character of the ads with the high energy and visual constraints of the 42nd

Product: Pfizer Corporate Headquarters, Lobby
Designers: Hixon Design Consultants
Creative Director: Kate Hixon
Client: Pfizer
Year: 2000

Product: Ernst & Young Headquarters, Window Display
Designers: Hixon Design Consultants
Creative Director: Kate Hixon
Client: Ernst & Young
Year: 2002

Product: IDEA
Designers: Hixon Design Consultants
Creative Director: Kate Hixon
Client: Anwei Law
Year: 1998

Street district ("razzmatazz" was actually specified in the design criteria). To bring these disparate sensibilities together, we turned the streetfront windows into infinity boxes and the Ernst & Young icons into white relief sculpture. The displays were then animated with changing colored light, and everyone was happy.

You do work for nonprofit organizations. What kind of work is that?
Primarily exhibition design and production, but also some branding and print. We have been working since 1995 for a group called IDEA (International Association for Integration, Dignity, and Economic Advancement). This work started as an awareness campaign for Hansen's disease. First was a photo exhibition at the United Nations and then a book, brochures, traveling exhibits, and now a headquarters and museum in Seneca Falls, New York. Their budgets are low, but we find the work rewarding; we get to enhance communication through design consistency.

Other nonprofit work includes various United Nations exhibitions, architectural signage for El Museo del Barrio, and an exhibit system for O2 (Green Design Networking Group).

Why do you do this nonprofit work?
Because I'm a hippie! I believe we all need to contribute to our world with whatever talents we are lucky enough to have been given.

When I first got started in the business, a lot of people gave me opportunities; now it is time to give back. Most of our nonprofit connections have some basis in academia or work at the United Nations. It gives us an opportunity to be with people who care about something—which is good for us as a group.

Product: United Nations
Designers: Hixon Design Consultants
Creative Director: Kate Hixon
Client: Doreen Beck
Year: 1999

Can you sum up your design philosophy in one word?
Context! Everything we do has a context. People ask me the
difference between design and art. Art creates its own context,
whereas design is always in reaction to something: a design brief,
a time span, a budget, an existing condition. Design is how to
make the most out of those ingredients.

Where do you get your ideas?
Again, it's context. Because context is why our solutions work.
It's where we get our ideas. All of our solutions and all of the
details in our solutions are linked. Our visual ideas come from the
analytical process we have learned at Pratt Institute. We lay out
what we are going to try to achieve, and we start to sketch
abstractly. Through that process an idea comes, we react to that
idea, and then we get another, and another, and another.

Product: El Museo del Barrio,
Architectural signage
Designers: Hixon Design
Consultants
Creative Director: Kate Hixon
Client: El Museo del Barrio
Year: 2002

Meaningful

DESIGNER: FRED BLUMLEIN

Title: President
Firm Name: Blumlein Associates, Inc.
Location: Greenvale, New York

You have been quoted as saying, "Design is about exercising your imagination." What do you mean by that statement?
Your imagination can be free only if you are free. When designing, we try to play; we laugh a lot. Silliness breaks down the adult in us.

What makes you happiest about being a designer?
It's about understanding the world—seeing what needs to be done, imagining what could happen, then expressing those ideas on paper and in models, then seeing it become reality and people using it. It's always a surprise to see people use the stuff because we think we had this particular intent and people use things any way they damn please. It's remarkable to see the ingenuity of human beings when they encounter your materials; the designs have a life of their own.

Computer-generated rendering of the Sony Comdex 2001 exhibit.

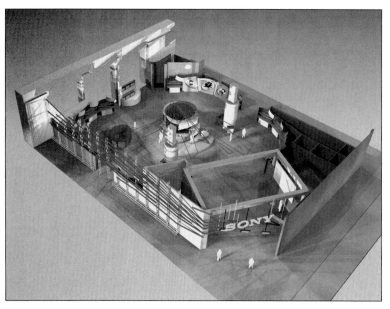

Why did you become a product designer?
I like the integration of graphics and environments. I have always considered the object to be an experience, a prop in the theater of life. What we do is come up with the environments that are the stages of life. Most of the founders of industrial design came out of the theater. Design is theater.

When did you know you wanted to be a product designer?

I had a wonderful teacher in high school who suggested I might have the talent to be a designer. I remember visiting Pratt and seeing a sewing machine that was different from anything I had seen before. As I was studying it, Rowena Reed explained how design was done in an understandable way. At that moment I knew that is what I wanted to do with the rest of my life. It was a eureka moment.

What's your favorite product?

The McPhone for AT&T is one of my favorites because it is ridiculous. It's a giant toy for grownups. It was commissioned by AT&T as part of a bakeoff among telecommunications companies to get the McDonald's account. We thought we could have some fun with it.

What is your favorite project you have done?

Both Spaceship Earth VIP Lounge for AT&T at Epcot Center and AT&T at the Movies Pavilion at Universal Studios were enormous fun to design and execute.

What are you working on now?

The Reckson Center for the Cradle of Aviation Museum on Long Island's Mitchell Field, where many planes were tested and pilots trained during World War II. We've been working on the Visitors Center and have just completed a restaurant called The Red Planet Café. It's a Mars station, a wacky environment themed to go along with the Cradle of Aviation Museum. The air and space museum has a remarkable collection of aircraft, including some of the Wright brothers' planes and a lunar module. We are supporting this with graphics and signage. It's wonderful to have a client who listens and appreciates ideas.

Final design concept of the Red Planet Café.

The main entrance of the 2001 Sony Comdex exhibit combined linear PVC tubing and digital graphic murals to create a sense of architectural space.

Can you sum up your design philosophy in one word?

Meaning! The meaning is the actual creation. The meaning is what people relate to in the spaces we create. The meaning is the people in the space. What will they need? How will they move through the space? What will their reactions be to the space? What do they smell, touch, feel in the space? Meaning exists on many levels. When we designed the History Bus for *Newsday* we created a series of interactive areas that fourth-graders can relate to and that can withstand their attack but with a depth of

The Sony Mobile Electronics exhibit at the 2000–2001 Consumer Electronics Show. The exhibit consisted primarily of digital graphic prints laminated to plywood. A mix of actual objects, including automobiles, was used.

meaning that adults can also enjoy. This is the challenge of exhibit design: layering meaning. As designers, we have to provide enough flexibility so the audience can find many meanings and each individual can have a unique experience. We seek a universality in the things we do so they hit a chord. We create experiences that go beyond language.

Initial concept sketch for the "Schooners and Steamships" exhibit module. The interior of the Winnebago housed five exhibit modules dealing with different areas of transportation

What qualifications do you look for in a designer?

One of the most stringent qualifications is humility. If you're going to be hired, you have to go through the test of being handed a broom and sent to the basement to clean up. A lot of people fail that test. I sweep and take the garbage out, and I expect everyone to do it. I also look for a sense of respect for other people's talents. Design is not about earning a living; it's about earning a life.

Can you describe your History in Motion project?

The Long Island paper *Newsday* did a series of articles looking back at the history of Long Island from the dinosaurs to the present. They wanted to bring this to children as a traveling exhibition in a 35-foot Winnebago and asked us how to do it. The content covered the history of aircraft, automobiles, boats, ships, and trains (the Long Island Railroad was the first commuter railroad in the United States). The exhibit travels to grade schools in New York State, where the fourth-grade curriculum is local history.

When you are designing for fourth-graders, do you design differently than you would for adults?

We work to make the exhibit, as the expression is, bulletproof because kids are going to jump on it, hang on it, and use it in ways you could not possibly imagine. Replacement is important,

Each History in Motion module had hands-on artifacts, such as steering wheels. When the artifacts were turned they caused interactive wheel graphics to rotate, revealing a series of informative visuals through "porthole" windows.

as well as simplicity. We made it easy for children to navigate, but for people who want to go deeper we added touch-screen interactives. These are on the outside as well, so people get a preview of what happens inside. The exterior design is also meant to entertain and inform even when it's just sitting still or driving down the highway.

What's your design process?

It's basically a communal effort. Everybody doodles, everybody has ideas, everybody has an opinion. When we start a project, we all sit around the table and throw out ideas. It's a community of ideas; usually we can't tell who came up with the ideas we eventually decide to develop. Laughing at what we are trying to accomplish helps us free our minds and explore areas we might reject if we are too serious. We put our egos aside and try to create something that's meaningful.

The Sony Mobile Electronics exhibit at the 2002 Consumer Electronics Show.

Question

DESIGNER: TOM HENNES

Title: Principal Designer
Firm Name: THinc Design
Location: New York City

What makes you happiest when you are designing?

I love the unsolved problem, which is much of the work we do in museums. The task of bringing unexplored territory to people who otherwise wouldn't likely encounter it is really fun and an enormous challenge. Most of our work goes beyond physical design to cognitive design.

So is it about bringing the story to the viewer?

It's beyond the story. It's the challenge of laying out a piece of terrain that people can explore in their own way. It's about giving people the chance to connect the dots themselves. We try to make the dots visible but let visitors do the work themselves so they have a role in the process instead of being passive passengers along a predetermined curatorial route.

Is this a new way of thinking about exhibit design?

I don't know if it's entirely new, but I think it's relatively unexplored. It runs counter to current trends in museum pedagogy, where the goal is for people to come away with a uniform result. We're taking an approach that embraces nonuniformity and embraces complexity and says people are capable of more than they are given credit for.

What's your most successful design?

One of our real mixed successes is the project we did for the Mystic Aquarium. I think it's successful because people do explore it; they do feel a sense of wonder, and many of them want to come back. It's a failure because it isn't sufficiently explorable. It's one of my favorites because it launched us on a whole new way of exhibit making.

Product: Challenge of the Deep
Client: Mystic Aquarium Institute for Exploration
Design Team: Tom Hennes, Bill Camp, John Evans, Sasha Marbury, Paul De Koninck, Daniel Maldonado
Fabricator: Mystic Scenic Studios, Spitz, Inc., The H.R. Hillery Company
Lighting designer/supplier: Paul Palazzo
AV designer/supplier: Xenon Pictures, Dennis Earl Moore Productions
Year: 1999
Photo: Jamie Padgett

Product: Nickelodeon Green
Slime Geyser
Client: Universal Studios,
Orlando, Florida
Designer: Tom Hennes
Year: 1992
Photo: Tom Hennes

Are people, in general, smarter than we give them credit for?

There's far too much seriousness about these things. I think the universe is a fantastically whimsical place. We're doing an exhibit about water for the California Academy of Sciences; it's the heart of an aquarium. The exhibit begins by addressing the connection between water and life. It turns out that life is an extension of processes that happen in ice. Water is constantly trying to be ice at 68 degrees, but then it remembers it's not supposed to be ice at 68 degrees. It's monstrously hilarious, mysterious, and stranger than anything you could make up. I don't know how we'll show that, but we'll get there.

Do you have a favorite project?

My favorite project is the Nickelodeon Green Slime Geyser because it's just a stupid machine that belches slime every fifteen minutes. This project is really about scatology; for kids.

Do you get to learn a lot doing exhibits?

Heavens, yes! It's a free education. We're doing a fantastic project with the Field Museum in Chicago that deals with the 15,000 years of human history in the Americas before the arrival of the Europeans. I've never done an anthropology project before.

How do you design? Where do you start?

There are as many ways of starting as there are projects. I'm torn between two approaches we use simultaneously. One is to gain enough sense of the material to get an intuitive feel, to make some leaps without getting lost in the subject, and the other is to dive deeply, to get lost in the subject and see whether that leap was the right one or not. It depends on when the magic strikes. Sometimes there's just a lot of fact and data gathering.

We talk a lot of the problems around; we sketch and scribble a lot. We have a wonderful collaborator, the sculptor Marc van ven Brook, who brainstorms projects. The two of us end up on the floor cutting pieces of paper and making funny models because something intuitive occurs to us. Sometimes those lead to insight. With Cal Academy we started doing very, very fast, rough cardboard models before we went into developing an explorable landscape. If you focus too much on the subject matter and too little on the exhibit material, you'd end up writing a wonderful textbook that you can't build. And if you focus too much on the physicality of the exhibit and the activities, you may miss some really interesting territory. We play with ideas as hypotheses and punch holes in them. If someone can't punch a hole after several rounds, we might have something worth keeping. Until an idea has gone through that process, it's just another idea.

Rainforest Cathedral Sketch

Who are your heroes?

My personal hero is John Dewey, who developed concrete executable criteria for experiences that are educative or noneducative, for defining what an experience is and how it actually functions. How you can use experience as a kind of positive good. How you foster experiences and open people to greater experiences. I continually go back to his slender little book *Experience and Education*, which has become our philosophical foundation and methodological, scientific approach. Now we're moving into areas he hadn't considered.

Can you sum up your design philosophy in one word?

Question. The quality of the exploration is only as good as the quality of the question. And explore, because if you stop looking at a place you haven't looked at yet, you're going to stop growing.

How did you become a product designer?

I did lighting and set design in the theater for several years. Then theater begot industrial shows that begot theme park attractions that begot an exhibition at Epcot. Though I was completely intimidated by doing an exhibit for IBM, by the end I was hooked.

The IBM exhibit at Epcot was a relaunching of IBM in the consumer eye. Paul Rand had done this spectacular rebus logo, which was the only thing in IBM's entire repertoire that had a wink to it. At first they didn't want to show it to anybody. Eventually we had a screen saver made of it that ended up on all

Product: Solutions for a Small Planet
Client: IBM
Location: EPCOT Innoventions, Orlando, Florida
Designers: Tom Hennes, Victor D'Alessio, Jim Goldschmidt, Jennifer Whitburn
Fabricator: Cinnabar, Orlando, Florida
Fabrication team: Dave Park, Barry Adamson
Lighting designer/supplier: Paul Palazzo
AV designer/supplier: Clarity

the Aptiva computers. The work on the exhibit started to infuse back into the brand as well. It's been wonderful to develop relationships with companies that are in a period of transition, because interesting things happen at those points.

What would you like to design if you could?
The mind fairly reels among submarines, gliders, helicopters, spaceships, and the Whalelarium where virtual whales swim up to you.

Product: Playstation Store at Metreon Center, San Francisco, California
Client: Sony Computer Entertainment America
Designers: Tom Hennes, Victor D'Alessio, Karen Gettinger, Miguel Petrusak
Year: 1999
Photo: Jean-Michel Addor

Product: Sony Playstation, E3 '97, Atlanta, Georgia
Client: Sony Electronic Entertainment
Designers: Tom Hennes, Victor D'Alessio, Sasha Marbury, Mike Graziolo, Daniel Maldonado, Dusan Mosscrop, Stephen Cook
Fabricator: Exhibit Group
Fabrication team: Chris Oberding
Lighting designer/supplier: Clarity
Year: 1997
Photo: Jamie Padgett, Ross Muir

Product: Seagate exhibit, Comdex '98, Las Vegas, Nevada
Client: Seagate Technology, Inc.
Designers: Tom Hennes, Rick Stockton, Dana Christensen, Marna Clark
Fabricator: Exhibitree
Lighting designer/supplier: Paul Palazzo
Year: 1998
Photo: Jamie Padgett

Chapter Nine

Corporate Design

Designing for corporations, large or small, means you are part of a corporate culture. Working for a corporation means you are designing for that specific company. The company is your client. In the automotive design area, that means you will design cars, trucks, and any other vehicles your company makes—but you will probably be a specialist. (In fact, this is true in most corporate design jobs.) You might, for example, work exclusively on big trucks. Be prepared to specialize!

Corporate design involves climbing the ladder to higher and loftier positions of design and design responsibility. You might start out as a team member on a large project and eventually be in charge of the creation and design of entire lines of automobiles or trucks. Many corporate designers remember wanting to design for the industry they are in when they were teenagers. Many top automobile designers knew when they were quite young that they wanted to design cars.

Furniture designers tell similar stories: "I just always wanted to design furniture." Discovering early that product design is what you want to do is very lucky. Being lucky enough to do it is wonderful. Designing for a specific industry—toys, furniture, tabletop, tires (yes, product designers do design tires), automobiles—is exciting and rewarding work because your designs are mass-produced. Corporate designers design and create products that influence the way people spend their time and money.

Although corporations may hire outside consultants, many employ a staff of designers responsible for large lines of products. Eastman Kodak has a large design staff for its cameras and peripheral products that is constantly challenged by new technology. Being on the inside has advantages; designers often work directly with scientists and engineers as they develop new and better technology. Having the inside track can put designers in the enviable position of creating and designing products that startle and change the world.

Designing for corporations is a fast-moving proposition; design assignments come quickly and furiously. Corporations must respond quickly to competitors' new offerings that threaten products they produce. Keeping ahead of the competition is another aspect of corporate design that makes it exciting and challenging. Corporate designers are asked to produce designs at lightning speed and under pressure from marketing and sales to do it right the first time. I'm not saying that most product designers don't work at a furious pace, but corporations have the kind of deadlines that can't be ignored. They need a certain product on time and deliverable.

Corporate designers are team players who work with a variety of professionals. They quickly get used to meetings; corporations like meetings to keep team members informed about and up to date on progress and schedules. Small corporations, however, may depend on the talent and creativity of a single designer.

As with all design jobs, staying in touch with what is new and what is next is vital. Traveling to conventions, trade shows, and just plain looking around is definitely a necessity for corporate designers. Management looks to them to predict the next direction the industry might take. Corporate designers live by the expression "who's hot and who's not." Looking, listening, observing, pondering, and then acting on those thoughts is a good approach for corporate designers. It's probably a good approach for any designer.

Beauty

DESIGNER: JON ZOGG

Title: Director, Corporate Design Group
Firm Name: Colgate-Palmolive Co.
Location: New York City

What inspired you to become a product designer?

I always loved to draw. An uncle was a graphic artist who illustrated travel posters and children's books. He was my first contact with a professional designer. I was interested in automobile design and walked into Pratt and met Bill Fogler, who took me on a tour, and I knew that was what I wanted to do.

One of the first designs I did when I came to Colgate was to increase the number of packages per case from sixty to ninety, increasing packing efficiency by 50 percent. Things get done for lots of reasons, and sometimes packaging efficiency drives a design.

Product: Dynamo 64 fl. oz. liquid detergent "Interlock 90" (I-90) shipping case design
Designer: Jon Zogg
Year: 1986

What is your favorite product?

My most recent product is my favorite; I got both the design and the mechanical patent for it. It's referred to as the FSSB, which stands for fabric softener, structural bottle. The bottle integrates aesthetic features and structural features that allow it to be produced with 20 percent less plastic. It's based on the folded-paper principle of structure; you gain rigidity by turning a surface on itself.

How do you integrate the graphics and the container?

When you are conceptualizing the container, you are thinking about the graphics. A good packaging designer is always aware of what's called the sweet spot, which is the center of gravity of the package where the logo often sits. As an industrial designer, you keep everything out of the way of the sweet spot. We are famous at Colgate for long names, so we have a particular challenge. Packages last for anywhere from ten to fifteen years, so the graphics change during the life of the product.

We redesigned the Octagon package to hold fewer ounces (from 48 to 40). By reducing the diameter and adding ripples to the grip area, we reduced the volume but also achieved a better gripping surface and maintained the graphics area. The grip sends a message to the user that it's easier to handle.

The Palmolive dishwashing liquid bottle is another example of developing a package from a material's point of view. We removed 20 percent of the material by switching from PVC to PET. The change in materials also had a positive environmental impact. I was then asked to integrate the four-touchpoint principle of packaging, which means that bottles touch at two high points and two low points all around. That allowed us to remove the corrugated dividers in the shipping box—a considerable savings in packing costs.

Formal family identity is part of every design brief, as are evolution and revolution. Can we be revolutionary, or do we remain evolutionary? Evolution picks up major cues from the previous generation, while revolution is used to revitalize a product and give it a new identity.

The soft soap bottle is an example of a revolutionary design. Jay Crawford, head of industrial design, came up with what is affectionately called the fishbowl design.

What is your most successful product?

The Ajax pack, created in 1985, is in every country of every size in the world. No other packaging has had that impact.

Product: Dynamo 64 fl. oz. liquid detergent—bottle design before (original right) and after redesign.

Product: Crystal White Octagon, redesign of 48 to 40 fl. oz. bottle. The downsize (circa 1985 and still on the market) keep the same height/size impression and adds a grip feature that further reduces volumetric content.
Designer: Jon Zogg

Product: Ajax Liquid Cleaner CSB Design
Designer: Jon Zogg
Photo: Colgate Corporate Communications

How would you define an industrial designer?

An industrial designer is a person who was destined to be an engineer but was afflicted with artistic talent along the way. You have to have a sense of how something is made. You have to know the materials to be able to manipulate them; you've got to know a material's limitations. Industrial design tends toward the artist more than the engineer because you can always find someone to engineer something but not necessarily to design it. It's a balance.

What's the role of the product designer?

It's the designer's role to determine what is obvious. We have to go through the dance, I call it. We have to go through all the motions of using the products we design. If you are designing a liquid detergent bottle, you have to take the bottle out of the closet, open the cap, put the cap down, pour the liquid, put the cap back on, and replace the bottle where you got it. Every movement is important. If you can anticipate those things, then the design is obvious. How people hold a bottle is very important. Do they hold it with four fingers? Do they grip it? Such simple actions determine what we design.

How do you design?

The company is constantly searching for new products to satisfy our customers' needs. Marketing comes up with a concept like "cleans teeth, freshens breath." If a new package is required, we get involved. We start out with the midsize pack in the family of packages. Some designers look at automobiles for ideas. We start sketching, create style boards, and try to emulate the feelings on the style boards. We zero in on one idea and put the hard edge to it; we make everything right—the handle, the label—making sure we have the sweet spot for the graphics. Then we make a full-size colored rendering. Interestingly, one of the things I've noticed is the more realistic you can make a conceptual idea, the more believable it will be for the nonartistic money people.

Product: Detergent family of products—Dynamo, Ajax, Fab, 32 and 64 fl. oz. bottle
Designer: Jon Zogg
Photo: Colgate Corporate Communications

Next we do volumetric models in clay. We have to know, when we are creating a 32-ounce bottle, that it actually holds 32 ounces. Now we can do this in the computer. Then we create a unit mold to create product for the marketing and engineering people for testing and packaging. Once that's approved, we start production molds. It takes, on average, one to two years to complete a project. We are constantly reemphasizing and selling the principles of design to nondesigners in the company.

What qualifications do you look for in designers?
Raw creativity with a sensitivity to order, design, balance, and aesthetics; also maturity; a sense of confidence. You can sense it in their handwriting.

What makes you happiest about your job?
What makes me happiest is to have the opportunity to use my creativity and to create a place where others can be creative.

Product: Windex 22 fl. oz. (Drackett Co.), redesign circa 1978
Designer: Teague Associates

Designers as Specialists

DESIGNER: JAMES MURRAY

Title: Design Director, Housewares, Tabletop
Design, Product Development
Firm Name: Federated Merchandising Group
Location: New York City

What was the most exciting thing you worked on recently?
We just finished the Linea ceramics project, which I term fast,
cheap, and out of control. In December a merchandiser in the
ceramics area asked us to do a modern, oversized lifestyle ceramic statement by a buy meeting in January. What a great opportunity! In no time I had two other designers working on twenty or thirty different iterations of each idea. As we finished the ideas, we handed them off to be rendered in the computer, and they were sculpted in foam

Product: Linea Corso
Designer: James Murray
Company: Federated Department
Stores
Year: 2002
Photo: Sinan Gundogdu

simultaneously. The whole thing was done within one week. As we
completed the drawings, we sent them to the buyers to confirm
that if we got it done by the meeting, they would buy it. We sent
the drawing and models to the manufacturer, and they shipped
back samples that were flawless just days before the meeting. The
ceramics were a huge success; the buyers bought twice what they
usually do with a new product line. This gives us a foot in the
door to bring in wood, metals, stainless steel, lighting pieces.

One fertile opportunity opens up, and we just flood it with the talent we have around here. If it does well, we'll build a whole lifestyle business around it.

How did the monkeypod wood line come about?

Actually, we started by picking up pieces of vintage teak from the 1960s that was sold by the Danish. We had nothing like it. We looked at some other beautiful exotic woods from Thailand, Indonesia, Malaysia, the Philippines. We settled on monkeypod because it was the closest to the tonality and look of teak we could find. There had been articles in some of the home magazines that teak was making a comeback in tabletop and furniture. What's nice about it is it's a different color than what's usually seen in department stores, and it's shape-oriented like the retro stuff. The buyers also went for it.

These are not your usual shapes; they look somewhat handcrafted. How was this done?

There is much more handwork with monkeypod wood products. Factories in the Philippines still do a lot of this kind of manufacturing by hand. Some of the general shapes are cut out by machine, but they do a lot of handwork to get the sculpted effects.

What is your favorite design?

I really loved doing Glasshouse. The idea was to get the picture out of a picture frame by floating the photograph between two pieces of glass and holding the glass out. We used nickel-plated wire to create the forms and let the glass float. You can actually put a flower in it. It moved picture frames out of the usual context.

Proline was unique because I challenged the vendor to do these high-domed lids with a porthole. You can see the food, but it's different from most cookware in both profile and how it functions. We used mostly a hard anodizing program, nonstick interiors, and oversized shapes, so proportionally it's really different. The stick handle looks like a stainless-steel handle, but it's actually stamped and pressed of really thick metal.

Product: Loft
Designer: James Murray
Company: Macy product development
Year: 1995
Photo: James Murray

Product: Proline
Designer: James Murray
Company: Federated Department
Stores
Year: 2002
Photo: Sinan Gundogdu

Product: Artemis
Designer: James Murray
Company: Federated Product
Development
Year: 1998

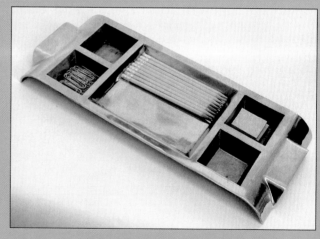

Product: Desk Organizer
Designer: James Murray
Company: Federated Department
Stores
Year: 1999
Photo: Sinan Gundogdu

Exciting

DESIGNER: VICTOR SANZ

Title: Industrial Designer, Corporate Design and
Usability
Firm Name: Eastman Kodak Company
Location: Rochester, New York

**What do you do every day that makes you happy you chose to
be a product designer?**
When you can look at a product and see a piece of yourself and
your vision in that product. Knowing that someone else will be
able to experience your vision and enjoy it, whether from a
functional aspect or a strictly aesthetic aspect.

In high school I saw pictures in magazines of these crazy
futuristic bikes. I thought they looked like sculpture with wheels.
It interested me to think about making functional art.

What inspired you to be a designer?
Form.

Why did you become a designer?
I wanted to be an artist, a painter, or a sculptor. I also wanted to
support myself. I figured that industrial design would be a good
way to get my sculptures into people's lives and make a living.

What were your early influences?
I looked at the work of a lot of artists such as Gaudi and saw how
they approached a problem differently. Making things that can be
static and boring into things that evoke interest, whether in a
good or a bad way, excites me.

Can you sum up your design philosophy in one word?
Exciting—because whatever you're doing will get a rise of
emotion, whether it's good or bad.

Product: 3.1 MP digital camera with a professional-quality Schneider-Kreuznach Variogon Lens, 4× optical zoom, 3.5× Advanced Digital Zoom, 14× total zoom
Designer: Kodak Corporate Design and Usability
Client: Eastman Kodak Company
Year: 2003
Photo: Victor Sanz

Simplicity

DESIGNER: JOHN CAFARO

Title: Director of Design for GM Full-Size Trucks
Firm Name: General Motors
Location: Detroit, Michigan

How would you describe what you do?
I create transportation for mass consumption; I design trucks. A truck embodies many aspects of industrial design.

Where do you start?
You start out looking at your past and the equity you have in your product, and you build on the strengths of that product. It's being honest, true, and very simple about the brand. Simple solutions in a truck are most successful.

How do you get ideas for trucks?
Designing a truck is a huge endeavor because GM invests billions and billions of dollars in huge manufacturing facilities. You have to look at the whole landscape of your business, and design is a big part of it. But how design integrates with the rest of the disciplines in the company is very, very important.

Product: 1997 Corvette
Designer: John Cafaro

Do you have a favorite design?
The most successful projects I've worked on were the ones where the aesthetic part of the solution really excelled. The design really stood on its own ground. The forms are beautiful and feel right. I'm most known for working on the current generation of the Corvette, which is a good study in the integration of high-performance functional parameters and beauty. I used everything I learned at school about three-dimensional form and design to shape that car. In the end, I had to put it in a wind tunnel and it had to perform. It was a very complex, very sculpted shape, and it was done

somewhat the old-fashioned way with tape, knives, and clay. But under the skin it's a technically sophisticated product.

Product: GMC Terradyne
Designers: John Cafaro,
GM Design Staff

So the Corvette was done traditionally. How does that differ from the new way?
We did a gorgeous full-size wood model to understand all the gaps and the fits. When you're using a lot of plastic components, you have to design for shrinkage and expansion of the material. Now we use math, design in the computer, and evaluate surfaces in virtual reality rooms. Though the tools of design are changing a lot, the emotion and the passion are still there. Design still has to be fun and intuitive.

Designing a Corvette is really emotional. That car is about emotion. Can you bring any of that to trucks?
We do that with trucks. Trucks have gone from the farmer's wagon to an image vehicle. They've become a fashion icon. Design plays a big, big role in how we market our trucks. With many brands and niches, some are very, very expressive; others are simply product-like.

When people buy a Cadillac truck, they expect a Cadillac.
The Cadillac truck has the look, feel, smell, and elegance of a Cadillac, yet inside it has the soul of a truck, whether it's pulling a horse trailer on a beautiful ranch or going out to a nice bed-and-breakfast.

Then there is the pickup truck.
The "Like a Rock" Chevrolet pickup has to be functional, simple to operate, easy to clean. The guy may take it out to the fair on a Saturday night, so it has to wash up well, like a cowboy.

Product: Cadillac EXT
Designers: John Cafaro, GM Design Staff

As an automotive designer, how do you get to know the client?
We do a lot of customer focus groups and listen to feedback from our customers, but as a designer you cherry-pick the information. You have to interpret it.

Do you show new product?
Sometimes the customer says a new product looks really wild, but he could get used to it in two or three years. You take that information back to the studio and develop it further. As the designer you are the visionary, and you can see seven or eight years down the road.
Developing concept vehicles for the auto show circuit is a big part of our job.

How did you discover automobile design?
I went to the 1967 World's Fair and the New York Auto Show, and the concept vehicles fascinated me. I wrote letters to GM, Ford, and Chrysler. They said go to Pratt. The fortunate thing is that I've been able to use some of the product design skill I learned at Pratt. The vehicles I've worked on have a little sense of the analytical product and less of the traditional Detroit zoom, zoom.

Can you sum up your design philosophy in one word?
I've learned that simplicity is one of the most important ingredients to good design. It's the key to timeless, lasting design. If you approach things in a simple, elegant fashion, they wear well over time. That's a proven formula.

Product: Hummer H2
Designers: John Cafaro, GM Design Staff

Product: Chevy Pickup
Designers: John Cafaro, GM Design Staff

Product: Avalanche
Designers: John Cafaro,
GM Design Staff

What advice would you give someone who wanted to be an automobile designer?

Automotive design incorporates all the disciplines, and everything has to work together. My advice is to really understand design in a holistic way, and you better love cars and business. The automobile business is a tough racket because design doesn't always play as big a role as you would hope. You have got to have talent. You have got to have a thick skin, and you have to be a student of design—architecture, ceramics, everything. That gives you an edge and a depth, and it prepares you for the long haul ahead.

Do you have a dream truck in your future?

We have some very expressive truck designs coming along. I think trucks will be classics twenty or thirty years from now because of design. The shapes are inviting and sensuous. I dream about a truck that's rugged but with the quality of some of the great cars. The Chevrolet SSR embodies a lot of what I'm talking about. The Avalanche and the Cadillac EXT have a level of innovation that nothing else has.

Product: SSR
Designers: Ed Wellburn, Executive
Director, GM Design Staff

Flexibility

DESIGNER: KEVIN OWENS

Title: Director, New Fun Stuff
Firm Name: Playworld Systems
Location: Lewisburg, Pennsylvania

What is your background?
Formerly, I worked at Water Entertainment Technologies (W.E.T. Design), Universal City, California, as a designer in WetLabs (an R&D facility). W.E.T. is a spinoff of Disney's Imagineering Group and creates permanent special effects in water, fog, and fire, usually for amusement parks and commercial or civic plazas.

So what does the Director of New Fun Stuff do every day?
I get to play catalyst among people who might not otherwise talk to each other.

What is product design, and how did you discover it?
Synthesizing function, appearance, user, market, engineering, and manufacturing while not dropping even one of the cats you've been juggling. Product design was the only path where it seemed

Product: Cityscapes and Ground Zero
Designers: Kevin Owens, Sachiko Uozumi, Eric Tritsch, Ian Proud, Greg Lannan
Creative Director: Kevin Owens
Year: 1998
Photo: Laurie Stahl

Product: Woodward ramps and rails by Huna Designs
Designer: Kevin Owens, Eric Tritsch, Wendy Frey, Nick Cipriani
Creative Director: Julie Karchner
Company: Huna Designs
Client: Huna Designs
Year: 2001 (ongoing additions)
Photo: Chris Hallman

possible to enjoy a career and life by having fun. Most people are afraid to really enjoy their work and career choices; our Puritan roots are showing.

What is your favorite design?
Ground Zero playground product line.

Where do you get your ideas?
Where don't I get my ideas!

Do you sketch or work three-dimensionally?
I work in three dimensions. My sketches are napkin-quality only. I don't make beautiful drawings.

What are you working on now?
I'm moving into pure trend research. I'm trying very hard to become not-a-designer. The time has come to pass the design torch on to others and move on to the next thing(s).

Product: The Galleon
Designers: Kevin Owens, Ricky Kline
Creative Director: Kevin Owens
Year: 1999
Photo: Phase I

Product: Cityscapes
Designers: Kevin Owens, Sachiko Uozumi, Eric Tritsch, Ian Proud, Greg Lannan
Creative Director: Kevin Owens
Year: 1998
Photo: Laurie Stahl

Chapter Ten

The Future of Design

What is the future of design? Many people think it can be found in three areas: universal design, green design or eco-design, and communication. Universal design, also called accessible or inclusive design, is a movement that started twenty-five or thirty years ago in architecture, when a vocal group of designers led by Ron Mace of the University of North Carolina designed homes that were wheelchair accessible. Universal design now encompasses a wide range of people involved in the design of products, interiors, communication devices, and architecture. Their interests range from the ageing to infants, from books to airports. Universal designers try to make products usable by the widest possible audience, by people of all ages and physical abilities. They stress the use of every sense—sight, hearing, smell, taste, touch, and plain old common sense—in the design of products. Universal design looks at the edges of the population rather than the middle, as has been the tradition in product design.

Henry Dreyfuss is credited with the creation of the first study of human factors in product design in the 1930s. His creation of Joe and Josephine as typical users of products helped direct and channel the statistical knowledge of human factors into the realm of the real person. But usually the data were for users in the middle 90 percentiles, which meant that anyone who fell into the top or bottom 5 percentiles wasn't included in the design process or was treated as a special case. Universal design looks to the extremes, the top and bottom 5 percentiles, to create products that can be used by everyone.

This is also true with respect to age. The elderly were discriminated against because it was thought they were not in the prime consumer categories. This is all changing as the population gets older. The older population is now seen as a powerful, wealthy, consuming group. Patricia Moore began her career as a product designer but is now considered one of the world's leading authorities on aging. Many designers practicing universal design have gone on to earn degrees in other areas of design, as they feel the need to explore this aspect of design's future more thoroughly.

Green design is the inclusion of the earth in any decision you make while designing. What effect will the design have on the environment? This is the question green designers ask. How will a product age? What effect will the materials it's made of have on the earth and the person using it? Is it safe? Is it biodegradable? Does the world need it? These are good questions, and many seem rather easy to answer. Green design, like universal design, is more an attitude rather than a series of guidelines. It's about respecting the earth and all life on it.

Recycle, reuse, repair are just a few of the words we all associate with green design, but it's much more complex than that. Manufacturing companies spend millions of dollars each year on green design that isn't evident to the average consumer. We are all aware that aluminum cans are recycled at a phenomenal rate, but are we aware of the furniture manufacturer that recycles its waste wood products into heat? Probably not, but the heat generated not only lowers the cost of manufacturing but also preserves the environment.

Green design is a transparent issue; when it works we are not aware of it, and when it doesn't everyone sees and feels the results. Designers can employ green design in many ways to have an effect on the ultimate product—for example, they can specify recycled materials and materials that are ecologically sound, use lumber that comes from regulated forests, remain aware of the effect materials

Jaime Salm's investigations into urban living and the disposable lifestyle of students led him to develop products that meet their needs without harming the environment.

have when placed in certain environments, and design products that last decades instead of years.

Many design firms now look at the effect a product will have on both users and the environment. This is just good design. Consumer products, by their very nature, are dangerous to the environment. The world consumes products; it's the way of our species. Changing this will take years of education and clarity and commitment on the part of designers. Some design firms are committed to this ideal and are setting standards many others will follow. Using postconsumer waste in the design of products remedies one situation but may lead to difficult design issues in the future when we become very good, as a society, at recycling. As green design becomes more and more a design issue, all designers will have to be educated in the full life cycle of a product, the cradle-to-grave theory of design. The product is only a small part of the design cycle; understanding the ramifications of green design, from raw material to waste, is the much larger scope of the product designer. Accepting this responsibility is just the beginning of the process.

Choosing to design a table of wood rather than glass may seem like a style decision, but it may not be if the designer considers all the ramifications of wood over glass. Wood develops a patina over time, whereas glass scratches and chips. The patina of the wood table speaks to us; the glass chips are annoying and dangerous. Wood can be recycled or even burned; glass is difficult to recycle and presents a hazardous disposal problem. If a designer is thinking green, the decision becomes much more complex.

Communication is part of the future of design because it is, in the end, what designers do. Designers communicate their ideas through form and the actions of products. More and more products communicate with us literally, through chips embedded in their workings. But that is just the latest development in product design. All products communicate messages through their form and material. A drinking glass made of crystal conveys a different message than one made of plastic. The materials, even when formed the same, express different ideas—the crystal through its luster, fragility, and heft, the plastic through its lightness and impermanence. The materials choices designers make send messages of wealth or efficiency.

Communication is the result of choices not only of material but also color, texture, and form. Add to these choices the probability that we will literally communicate with the products that surround us, and the possibilities abound. Communication permeates the process of design from ideation to sketches to prototypes to discussion to interviews to production. It may be the single most important aspect of what product designers do. We may, in fact, be more communicators than anything else. Wendy Brawer discovered a new way to communicate with her green maps, which identify all the green places in cities. Jaime Salm's investigations into urban living and the disposable lifestyle of students led him to develop products that meet their needs without harming

Wendy Brawer discovered a new way to communicate with her green maps, which identify all the green places in cities.

the environment. Patricia Moore wrote a book called *Disguised* about how the elderly are treated in North America. They are opening new areas for designers to explore and learn from.

Universal design, green design, and communication are the future of design because much of the research about design is done in these areas. They are new, exciting, and full of contradicting points of view. If you are interested in changing the world, these are the areas of design to pursue.

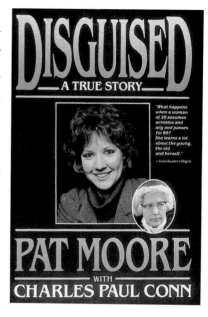

Interconnection

DESIGNER: WENDY E. BRAWER

Title: Director
Firm Name: Green Map System
and Modern World Design
Location: New York City

What's your most recent project?

Solspherica is an interactive solar exhibit in Liberty Science
Center in Jersey City, New Jersey, that I designed in collaboration
with Amelia Amon of Alt. Technica. The three-year project won a
design competition that the Art and Science Collaborations put
together with Liberty Science Center. It's based on the compass
and has four elements that help young people understand the
practical and lyrical power of solar energy: earth, home,
community, and the galaxy. We used a solar-powered theremin
because we felt it creates the music of the stars. Solspherica was
constructed on the roof of the Science Center so you have a view

Product: Solspherica
2000
Designers: Amelia Amon,
Wendy E. Brawer
Company: Alt. Technica
& Modern World Design
Client: Liberty Science
Center
Year: June 2000
Photo: Wendy E. Brawer

Product: Solspherica 2000
Designers: Amelia Amon,
Wendy E. Brawer
Company: Alt. Technica &
Modern World Design
Client: Liberty Science Center
Year: June 2000
Photo: Wendy E. Brawer

of the community and a house, which represents the home of the solar system. It shows how your home would light up if it were wired for solar energy, and it's got a solar tracker on the solar cells that's controlled by the young people, so they can see how important the alignment with the sun is. We used as many recycled and renewable materials as we could, but because it's outdoors, we had to use some plastics and very durable materials.

Your goal was to teach children about solar energy. Why do you think this is important?

North Americans use more than 25 percent of the world's energy, but we are less than 5 percent of the world's people. That we are using 300 million-year-old fossils for energy instead of relying on today's solar power is causing enormous problems. We produce a huge amount of carbon dioxide: we create wars and inequities all over the world because of our choice of energy. So as designers we wanted young people to see what options exist and learn that some are more appropriate than others. A science museum should help kids understand the potential that exists now as well as possibilities for the future.

Why did you choose to become a green designer?

There had always been an element of green design in my artwork even before I thought of myself as a designer. In 1989 I began thinking seriously about product design, and the first thing I wanted to make was a watch that counted down to the turn of the century. I went to Hong Kong to the National Watch Show to talk to a manufacturer about it. From there I went to Bali for vacation, and I could see things were disappearing in this incredibly beautiful place. I realized that my creative energy could be turned toward things that would help stop this disappearance and help people connect with their unique environment. I knew I could speak to people about that.

Why green, rather than social responsibility?
We are in a period of rapid extinction. I want to help change the way we think about the way we live—the delicacy and interconnectedness of how we live. I'm interested in longevity and legacy.

What is your design philosophy in one word?
Interconnection. Everything is interconnected. As designers, we have to understand that we live in a web—whether it's an info web, a web of life, or a web of relationships. Everything you do impacts something else. If we were conscious of those interconnections, of who or what might receive the inadvertent outcomes of what we do, we might change what we do and how we do it.

What is your favorite project?
The Times Square Recycling Bin. As a member of the Manhattan Solid Waste Advisory Board, I proposed a public space recycling bin where people could deposit bottles and cans and others could redeem them. The self-emptying bin dignifies the process and makes it safe by raising the bin to eye level so the person can reach in without bending over. The bins are made of 20 percent recycled material, so that sends a complete message.

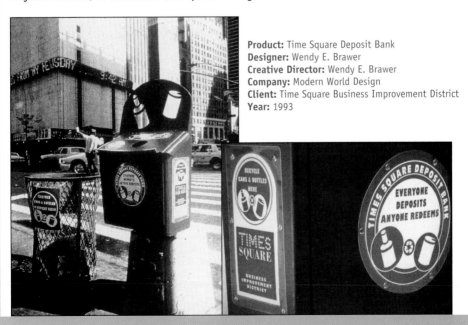

Product: Time Square Deposit Bank
Designer: Wendy E. Brawer
Creative Director: Wendy E. Brawer
Company: Modern World Design
Client: Time Square Business Improvement District
Year: 1993

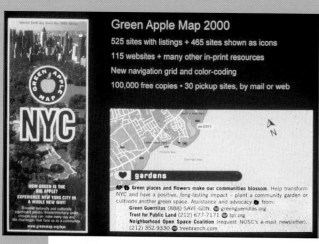

Green Apple Map 2000

525 sites with listings + 465 sites shown as icons

115 websites + many other in-print resources

New navigation grid and color-coding

100,000 free copies • 30 pickup sites, by mail or web

gardens

Green places and flowers make our communities blossom. Help transform NYC and have a positive, long-lasting impact – plant a community garden or cultivate another green space. Assistance and advocacy from:

Green Guerrillas (888) SAVE-GDN, greenguerrillas.org
Trust for Public Land (212) 677-7171 tpl.org
Neighborhood Open Space Coalition (request NOSC's e-mail newsletter).
(212) 352-9330 treebranch.com

Green Map System Icons
Systeme d'Icônes Cartographiques Verts

Iconos del Sistema de Mapas Verdes
グリーンマップシステム・アイコン

Product: Green Apple Map 2000
Designer: William van Roden
Creative Director: Wendy E. Brawer
Client: Green Map System, Inc.
Year: 2000
Photo: Beth Ferguson

How did the green maps come about?

The green maps originated in 1992 on the day I learned that 2,000 folks were expected at the United Nations for five weeks to plan the Earth Center. That got me thinking about all the great green things happening all over New York. That same day I came up with the name "The Green Apple Map" and arranged for printing. That map got a lot of attention because it presented a view of New York that had been invisible until then.

The green map came out of a need to create a promotional service for the environment. After the second edition, people asked if they could create a similar map for other cities. That's how the idea grew. We ended up creating green icons for the maps designed by kids and professionals. We also created stickers for people without computers. The idea of creating a font came later. The icons help people think about the types of information they're going to show.

People all over the world have taken ownership of the green map project; seventy maps have been published so far. Altogether, thirty universities are using green map projects as part of the learning experience. We are the clearinghouse for the Green Map System.

Green maps are portable, lightweight, resource-efficient, and have this incredible power to personalize a place. Everybody starts to look at where they live, work, or go to school in a different way. When you think about how to make a green product—what are good materials that have a good message and use decentralized production—for something that's got local importance that makes a difference, the green map is hard to beat.

What's next?
Many more collaborative efforts. So many more products are needed. How can I help designers find a light switch to turn them on? I hope to be able to stay aware enough to make more things happen. I want to teach more.

Empathy

DESIGNER: PATRICIA MOORE

Title: Design Director
Firm Name: MDA
Location: Phoenix, Arizona

Why did you start your own company?
When I emerged from nearly four years experiencing life as elders, and writing my book, *Disguised*, companies inundated me with requests to help them understand the agenda of inclusive design for all, for the lifespan. How could I say no? If I have a frustration about what I do with my consulting, it is that I've been a bit like BASF: I don't make the thing, I make it better. The majority of my work has involved changing corporate cultures to do more inclusive design. It's like trying to identify the glass of water I've poured into the ocean!

Product: Interior of Canadaair
Designer: David Ellies
Year: 1980
Photo: Patricia Moore Design Association

How did you come up with the idea that started the company?
I just knew in my head and heart that exclusive design—design for the fittest—eliminated the majority of consumers and their precious wants and needs. I truly believe we are only as strong as the weakest link in the chain. Knowing that there were products and places that couldn't be utilized by a majority of people made absolutely no sense to me, either pragmatically or emotionally.

Why gerontology?
Because a senior designer at Loewy once turned to me in a review meeting and pronounced, "We don't design for those people, Pattie!" They were referring to the consumers I was

REHAB BY DESIGN

always focusing on: people living with the effects of illness, injury, birth anomalies, and the normative changes of late life. I wrote a memo to Loewy and asked for permission to split my time between my responsibilities at the office and grad school: biomechanics at New York University, psychology and counseling at Columbia; gerontology at Columbia. I knew I had to be able to speak a multitude of languages if I were going to be able to communicate the concept of universality, inclusivity, through design.

We all are getting older. How can design help us age gracefully?

How can we age gracefully *without* the support of good design? Design should enhance ability, not remind someone of what they

Product: Independence Square Rehabilitation Centers
Designers: Patricia Moore, David Guynes
Year: 2000
Photo: Patricia Moore Design Association

can no longer do or never could do. Design should not present risk or potential for harm. Design should embrace each user and his or her individual ability, like a mother's hug of pure love and acceptance.

Why design products for the elderly?
The same reason I like to design for infants, toddlers, and young children: they need good design the most.

You have been involved in universal design and accessibility for years. Has the design field responded to designing for the elderly?
Designing specifically for late life presents a finite range of needs and opportunities. The prospect of universality, in all environmental and product design, addresses the potential of usability for the lifespan, regardless of age or ability. The design community hasn't fully embraced the inevitable challenge of considering all consumers as equal in their right, their need, for places and things that encourage their happiness and satisfaction. As the boomer cohort is approaching sixty years of age, I have faith that they will present a unified voice for accommodation.

Product: Patricia Moore with a mockup of a mobile ray X-ray unit
Designer: Chuck Mauro
Year: 1980
Photo: Patricia Moore Design Association

How can designers become involved in universal design?
All design should be universal, inclusive of the needs of all users as equal, supportive of individual requirements.

What products have you been involved in designing that epitomize good design?
OXO Good Grips have emerged as an icon of universality, and it was a delight to work on this project from its inception with Sam Farber and Davin Stowell. And so much of what I've worked on in health

maintenance and medical diagnostics, particularly full-body tomography, mammography, dialysis. I am also tremendously proud of the fully accessible vehicle design for the new Greater Phoenix Light Rail System, which is a current project.

How do you work? How do you attack a design problem?
Immersion; empathy; assimilation. I always use the information the client gives us as the basis for confirming or altering their assumptions, and then we get started with research to support the range of concepts and outcomes that will address the opportunity.

Do you have a favorite client or design experience? Describe something that was a surprise at the end.
From 1990 through 2000 I was focused on creating unique environments for the delivery of physical rehabilitation for pediatrics, geriatrics, industrial injuries, and general physical medicine and rehabilitation. Working with patients and their families helped redefine my passion for inclusive design solutions. Every day was full of not mere surprises but true miracles of medicine and faith in unison.

Do you do a lot of research? Focus groups?
I have never worked on a project that hasn't included research. Our methodologies are the distinction of our practice. They involve the full realm of social science and business tools and approaches, with our unique twist. I insist that empathy be utilized in all projects. This applied experience produces corporate conversions that have totally reoriented projects, their scopes, and budgets. I once was asked by a Fortune 100 health care company to conduct a focus group for caregivers for elders with incontinence. The client admitted afterward that they were assuming their primary consumer would be frail elders. The actual focus should be any woman who has borne a child and women in perimenopause or menopause. Nothing feels better than achieving an unexpected success.

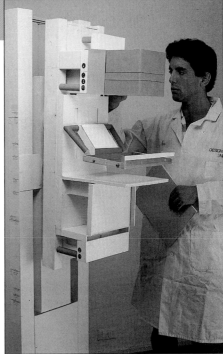

Product: Mock-up of the LoRAD Mammographic Unit
Designer: Patricia Moore
Year: 1987
Photo: Patricia Moore Design Association

Executive from a pharmacy chain in an empathic exercise
to evaluate his experience functioning in one of his
stores with reduced capacity.
Photo: Patricia Moore Design Association

**When you are designing, how do you work?
Do you mock things up in your shop?**
It's a combination of absorbing written
materials, observation, empathy,
sketching—yes, with paper and
pencil—making mockups, testing, and starting
the cycle all over again till we get it right!

**Do you have a few words of wisdom for
people starting their own design business?**
I am a passionate promoter of niche marketing.
Find a void. Fill it. Reinvent the wheel. Make a
better mousetrap. March to your own drummer.
Never leave well enough alone!

**Can you sum up your design philosophy in
one word?**
Empathy. The only way I can honestly create
solutions for everyday living, for everyone's
lifestyle, and for all people's lifespans is by
understanding what they want, need, and
dream.

Collaboration

DESIGNER: CHRISTIAN P. ARKAY-LELIEVER
Title: Director of Product Development
Firm Name: Skidmore, Owings & Merrill LLP
Location: New York City

What is your favorite product?
Lizardman, because I was able to adapt it from nature. And the time was right. The end product evolved from the manufacturing process and the design brief, which was to look for your inspiration. I also like that the stool has character. When I design, I look for the character in a product. It gives the product life.

Who are your heroes?
Davis Allen, especially since I work at SOM. His designs demonstrate the importance of keeping the design integrity of the space. The spaces and products he designed are one. Phillippe Stark, because his character and imagination come out in the products he designs. They may not be functional, but they are very creative, and that's what people respond to. Jordan Moser, because he designs products and spaces as one; that's what makes him special.

What is the design process at SOM Collaborative like?
It's rigorous! The process is collaborative, as the name implies. The 1,200 people at the firm have 1,200 ideas each! We had to develop forums for the exchange of ideas to give everyone a voice. No idea is too out there! We look at everything. SOM was and is a pioneer in the business of architecture and product design. We are always developing new concepts and questioning how people live and work.

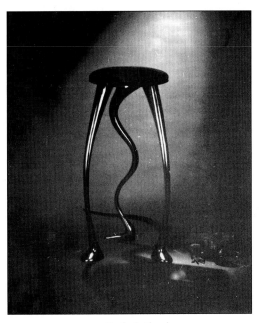

Product: Lizardman
Designer: Christian P. Arkay-Leliever
Year: 1993
Photo: Yves Malo

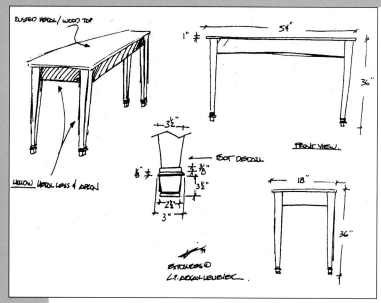

Product: Exposures
Design: Christian P. Arkay-Leliever
Year: 1998

What is it like to design in an architectural environment?

Something is always going on. This is a big firm with lots of clients—from hotels to major office buildings. We try to custom design everything to fit our clients' specific needs. Each architect has great ideas, which we try to support. We try to harness the ideas and develop them for general sale.

What kind of products do you design?

Anything that has to do with a space: case goods, furniture, wardrobes, lighting, textiles, bath products, hospitality products for hotels. We are always looking at what the users of a product do and how that use can be improved.

How did you discover product design?

In high school I was interested in neon signs. I found a manufacturer in Toronto. I had a drawing I wanted to have made

Product: Exposures
Design: Christian P. Arkay-Leliever
Year: 1998

in neon. I was working at a glass store where the idea started, so I cut the glass and took it over to the manufacturer, and they helped me make it. They taught me how to bend neon. Then a local store put my work on display. It was the first time I drew something, got it made, and put it on display. That's when I knew I wanted to do product design.

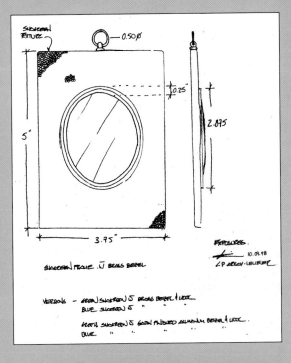

Product: Hope Frame—"Jewels et Gems"
Design: Christian P. Arkay-Leliever
Year: 1998

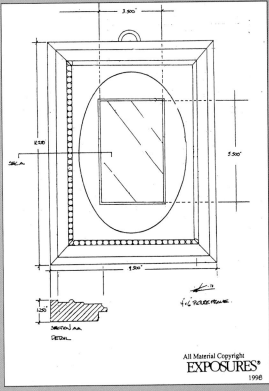

Responsible Desire

DESIGNER: JAIME SALM

Title: Principal Designer
Firm Name: MIO
Location: Philadelphia, Pennsylvania

How did you discover industrial design?
I used to make sculptures out of metal found in junkyards in towns near Medellin, Colombia, where I am originally from. This was the result of years of art classes, workshops, a supportive family, and an architect who was my mentor at the time. Sculpture taught me how to think in three dimensions and helped me discover the importance of persistence. One of my teachers suggested I look into industrial design as a profession. I saw it as an opportunity to continue my sculpture work under the strongest constraints in creative endeavors: function and people. Design as a mental activity is initially discovered in the classroom and then as an approach to life all around you. Design becomes a way of channeling, editing, and giving shape to information in its most relevant form: a complex language with infinite variables. Discovery of design is a gradual process that never ends. This means that I have not fully discovered design. I hope to enjoy its discovery forever.

Jaime Salm and Tangent

How do you define green design?
Green design is more than evaluating resources, their origin and life cycle, to understand and quantify their impact. Green design can ultimately explain the relationships between people and products. To design responsibly today,

Product: Stoop
Designers: Jaime Salm, Daniel Kushner, Michael Andrulewich
Photo: Robert Hakalski

one has to stretch existing infrastructures and strategies to bridge conventional business practices and ideas with sustainable development and design. Taking into account the full life cycle of a product and its participants (those affected directly and indirectly by the design), green designs answer the following questions: What is the real product (service)? How should it be made (offered)? Who is it for? And why should it exist? The questions seem easy enough, but when the product is observed throughout its life cycle, thousands of design issues become evident. The purpose of green design is to consider and solve as many of those issues as can be controlled by the designers without reaching a point where the product will never make it to market. At the same time it is essential for green design to be desirable, beautiful, elegant, and democratic. Green design is not green if it is not viable. Its success depends on its ability to shift people's perceptions of value. Products must educate with desire, a language that is familiar to consumers, and one that, if carefully crafted, can generate a new set of values based on awareness and information leading to a new level of intelligent consumption. I would call this state responsible desire, which is the perfect hybrid of our current sociocultural and economic systems with an injection of new values.

Product: Grid It
Designers: Jaime Salm, Daniel Kushner,
Michael Andrulewich
Year: 2003
Photo: Robert Hakalski

How do you work?

My design process relies on understanding people, their
behaviors, their environments, and the culture they generate. The
answers to most design problems can be found in everyday life.
Finding the appropriate design opportunity and making it viable
is the focus of the process. A diverse team of collaborators makes
seeking the answers easier. There are no set formulas to design,
but there are stages that are helpful in maximizing design time.
We mold the process around the needs of each project. The best
way to generically describe my design process is as follows.

Every design starts with a project brief definition stage and a
broad research phase. The project brief is written or rewritten in
the simplest and clearest manner possible. A timeline is
established and deadlines are determined. Key ideas and topics
are listed and distributed among the researchers. Each researcher
leaves the studio with a camera and a timeline to collect
information relevant to the brief. Once all the information has
been collected, it is presented in refined opportunity categories.
At this point, everyone selects a point of entry and produces
sketches, models, prototypes, and presentations of a few
concepts. The best are selected and refined in teams for a second
presentation. One idea is chosen and shown to potential
developers for evaluation. The concept is corrected based on the

evaluation, and a prototype is made. The concept is tested and carefully analyzed. After a second round of adjustments, the concept is ready for production.

Why are you designing green products?
I am designing products the way I learned to design them. Sustainability was not taught as a separate subject at my school. The environmental, social, and cultural impact and role of my projects are not afterthoughts or side issues. Selling greenness is a dangerous business; selling performance and intelligence will always give you an advantage. Until performance values shift and legislation embraces greenness, the best way to design green is to design stealthy green: slick, affordable, functional—and by the way, it's also green.

Product: Fibrid Bowls
Designers: Jaime Salm, Daniel Kushner, Michael Andrulewich
Client: Fibrid
Year: 2001
Photo: Fibrid

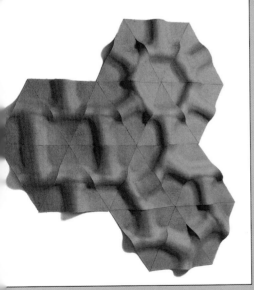

Product: Tangent
Designers: Jaime Salm, Daniel Kushner, Michael Andrulewich
Year: 2003
Photo: Robert Hakalski

Is it important that the consumer be aware of green design? How do you tell the story of your products and that they are good for the environment?
It is important for consumers to become aware of and respond to the current state of product culture, but I believe it cannot be achieved through brute force and traditional environmental marketing. Environmental information is not easy to understand. Environmental awareness needs to cloak itself with responsible desire to become a viable, mainstream voice in the values of consumers. This voice is currently being partially embraced even without its most sophisticated masks, which leads me to think there is an opportunity for designers and businesses to become aware of, create, and profit from a more sustainable economy.

I am currently working on launching a new line of products, and I am finding the best way to begin to create this culture of responsible desire is to make the consumer a partner. We are starting by sharing basic information about the company about the products—why they should exist and how they are relevant. The idea is to slowly increase the amount of information, educating the consumer on new ways to understand, judge, and enjoy products.

Can you sum up your design philosophy in one word? Why?
Responsible desire. Design is too powerful a tool to be used indiscriminately.

Chapter Eleven

Design Entrepreneurs

Starting your own company is the dream of many designers. Creating products that sell while continuing to create products they think the world needs is the goal of many designers. Starting a company and designing the products is the way many huge corporations started. Every field has great entrepreneurial stories. Usually these businesses start in a garage or basement and because of the success of the products become large companies. Corporations sometimes create entrepreneurial areas that nurture creativity and new products. These have been called everything from

Skunkworks to Barns. The designers who work in them are usually left alone to think and create. All sorts of new products and ideas come from these establishments.

Many designers who start their own manufacturing companies do so out of frustration with manufacturers or because no one believes in what they have designed. Being a product designer and staying in the business of product design is hard enough; now add to that the complications of manufacturing and distribution. Why would anyone do this? Usually it is just in the designer's soul. He or she just wants to make something that is better or more beautiful and to produce it personally. It's also about control. Design entrepreneurs get to control not only their design but also the manufacture of their design. It gets made the way they want it to be made. The process is controlled from concept to packaging to distribution. Usually these businesses start as a sideline to the ongoing business of design and mushroom and take over the designer's life.

Craig Vetter wanted to make a thing called a fairing for motorcycles. He just thought it was a good idea to create a shield that protects the motorcycle rider from the wind at 60 miles per hour. A simple idea. But who would have thought it would be a giant success?

Design entrepreneurs do what most designers do well—they observe—but then the entrepreneurs act on their observations. They often get involved in designing stuff they need for themselves. Yes, design is the mother of invention. Someone makes something and then someone else says, "I could use one of those!" That's the beginning. Pretty soon the designer is making a short production run, next he's selling the products not just to friends and acquaintances but on the Internet or at conventions or motorcycle races. While there is no one way design entrepreneurs get started, they do all eventually have to create business plans, hire people, and do just about everything anyone else does who starts a new business.

Design entrepreneurs work in every field of design, from furniture to toys; there are no limits. Each field demands the same thing: a belief that what the designer designed is a terrific idea and that the world needs it.

Doing More with Less

DESIGNER: CRAIG VETTER

Title: Designer
Firm Name: Vetter Design Works, Inc.
Location: Carmel, California

You started your company in a garage, designing stuff for yourself. How did it grow so large?
When I graduated from the University of Illinois in 1965, I interviewed at the big design houses, but I couldn't find anyone doing what I wanted to do. Because of the influence of Buckminster Fuller, I had become convinced that in the future we would have to do more with less.

   Motorcycles did more with less, and it was easy to support myself by hopping up motorcycles. It was on my 305 cc Yamaha in Kansas, en route to the 1966 Aspen IDCA, that I realized I could design fairings, those slippery aerodynamic cowlings that make riding more comfortable while offering better mileage.

What was the first product you made?
By Christmas 1966 I had made a half dozen or so fairings, all for friends' bikes. I decided that my name, Vetter, was as good as anything for my company, I designed my logo, and I began to run ads in motorcycle magazines. Riders from around the world began to take a chance and order the "Series 1000 Vetter Fairing."

How did you know you were onto something big?
I just knew. It was a period of rapid growth in motorcycles, with the Japanese upping the ante every year in engine size and sophistication and me upping it with them. Between 1966 and 1971 I designed seven beautiful fairings,

Product: Windjammer Poster
Designer: Craig Vetter
Year: 1977
Photo: Craig Vetter

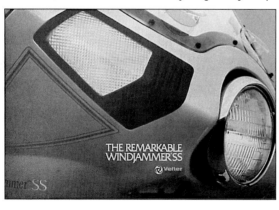

each for a specific motorcycle size and each made of hand-laid fiberglass. These were great fairings but poor products; no dealer could afford to stock them along with everything he needed. So in 1971 I began with a fresh sheet of paper and designed the Windjammer, a fairing designed to be made and sold—a good product—while still being a wonderful wind protector. The Windjammer, introduced in April 1971, was the right thing at the right time.

Product: 1978 Windjammer SS
Designer: Craig Vetter
Year: 1978
Photo: Craig Vetter

What was your favorite product you manufactured?

The Windjammer SS of 1977—its most refined form still is the most classically beautiful fairing ever made. It's what happens when a designer is in charge of what a company makes.

How did you happen to design racing wheelchairs?

By 1978 I had pretty much exhausted my ideas about what to do for motorcycles. Besides, it looked as if the factories would be putting out their own fairings. It was time to sell. I bought an ultralight powered Pterodactyl. Unfortunately, on takeoff, a dust devil approached from behind and slammed me into the ground, breaking both of my legs. When I got out of the hospital, I cut up the Pterodactyl and turned it into a wheelchair.

Product: Craig Vetter sitting in the Equalizer T-2 wheelchair
Designer: Craig Vetter
Year: 1981
Photo: Craig Vetter

Wheelchairs in 1980 were heavy contraptions that were almost impossible for the user to tuck into the rear seat without help. Besides, they made you look sick. I set out to design a human-powered vehicle that solved the problems I knew firsthand. My Equalizer T-2 of 1981 got you noticed for the right reasons—you looked cool. When they allowed wheelchairs to compete in the Boston Marathon in 1982, Jim Knaub used my design to beat the runners, thus exemplifying the ultimate more with less.

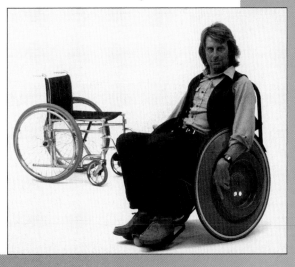

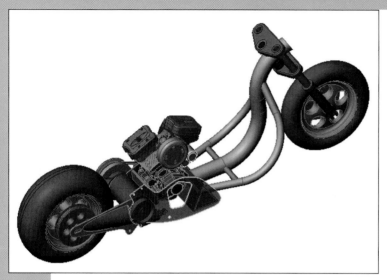

Product: Defiant Scooter
Designer: Craig Vetter
Year: 2002
Photo: Craig Vetter

You're now working on a giant scooter? Why?

As we move through life we have different interests, different needs. I have always designed for my time in life. I am now sixty years old. I want a scooter. For some unknown reason, people have always thought of motor scooters as being tiny. Not me.

Motor scooters are easy to get on and off because you don't have to throw your leg over anything. You simply sit down and ride away. Plus, you can carry more on a motor scooter and streamline it better. I decided to make such a vehicle for myself, with the probability that my aging baby boomer generation would also be attracted to it. I hope to up the ante to 100 miles per gallon, ride it cross-country, and have fun. The goal is still to do more with less.

When you're designing, how do you work? Do you mock things up in your shop?

I have never worked for anybody. I work alone in my workshop, designing and building my dream. The design of the Defiant pretty much represents the process: A businessman friend heard me talking about this giant motor scooter and offered to organize a company to develop and produce it. I began by rearranging Harley Heritage parts into a motor scooter, mocking up the frame in plywood and plastic pipe. Then I had metal fabricators turn this model into metal. I assembled the components and drove the scooter all summer in 2002. I learned what was wrong and what was right about it. But, most important, I knew I wanted a big motor scooter like this. I'll be riding the second model soon. Production will probably always be from digital files and be small.

Product: Wood and cardboard mockup
Designer: Craig Vetter
Year: 2003
Photo: Craig Vetter

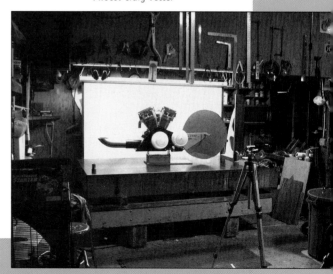

What is product design?

I list all the things a product must do. Tops on the list is how it will be marketed. If I cannot figure out how to market it, I abandon the idea early on. The solution should continue the tradition of doing more with less.

What is your favorite design? Why?

When I made my first fairing in 1966, motorcycles got 40 miles per gallon (mpg). Cars got 15. By 1980, many cars could get 40 mpg while motorcycles were still getting 40 mpg. I decided to host the Craig Vetter Fuel Economy Contests in the 1980s to determine the upper limits of fuel economy of street vehicles at real highway speeds. Between 1981 and 1985, mileage went from 100 mpg to 500 mpg. Wow! Isn't that doing more with less?

What would you like to design if you could? Why?

I want to design and host a new series of contests to encourage the development of air scooters—small, personal flying vehicles. I have designed a contest that will lead to safe, usable transportation. I need sponsors to make it happen. Successful, safe personal flying machines will change the world.

Product: 1973 Triumph Hurricane
Designer: Craig Vetter
Year: 1973
Photo: Craig Vetter

Can you sum up your design philosophy in one word?

Doing more with less. Why? We do not have to fear the future if we do more with less. The future is ours.

Simplify

DESIGNER: JOEL DELMAN

Title: Designer
Firm Name: Product Development Technologies
Location: Chicago, Illinois

How did you discover industrial design?
It was a cold winter day in Boston, my first year of law school, and I stumbled across a funny magazine called *ID*. At that moment for the first time in my life I knew what I wanted to do when I grew up.

How do you work?
Each design project is different, and there are many ways to approach a problem depending on the solution sought. Is the client just looking to reskin an existing object, or do they want to rethink the way it works, the way a user experiences it? Even if the former is the goal, can we sneak in some good thinking anyway?

That leads me to a cardinal rule of design: I never pick up a pencil to draw before I start to think—really think—about the problem. And when I do pick up that pencil, it's an extension of my mind as well as my eyes. Making something look cool is the easiest part of industrial design. But it's the ability to inform product designs with knowledge that sets designers apart from the competition, that permits them to exceed their users' expectations for functionality and innovation, and that forms the foundation on which any good design solution must be built.

I gather as much information as possible about the product, its end users, its competitive environment, and technologies that might influence its functionality before I start playing with

Product: Bubblin' Glitter Fish
Designer: Joel Delman
Company: Twenty Twenty Thinking
Client: Little Kids, Inc.
Year: 2000
Photo: Tanya Sillitti

aesthetic possibilities. To the extent truly new ideas are needed, focused lateral brainstorm sessions with the design team always create opportunities the client never dreamed of. Then, once the foundation has been laid, two-dimensional sketching and three-dimensional form explorations work hand in hand to bring ideas to life. Refinement takes place over at least two phases (with input from the client throughout) until the optimal solution is achieved.

Product: Psyclone 90 Go-Kart
Designers: Gil Canada, Donna Piacenza, Jean Kiple, Joel Delman
Company: Product Development Technologies, Inc.
Client: Karts International, Inc.
Year: 2002
Photo: PROE Rendering by Mark Gartz

Designing consumer products must be a challenge, given the high volumes and design constraints.

Design constraints imposed by mass manufacture and marketing requirements do limit creative choices and influence decisions in ways that can sometimes be frustrating. But it's those same constraints that make the task interesting. Sometimes you need a box to push against in order to achieve great results; without the walls I'd get lazy.

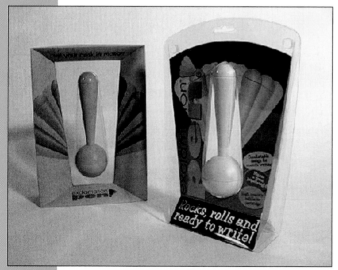

Where do you get your ideas?

I love to walk. I make a conscious effort to remain aware of the world around me in an energized way. Inspiration can sneak in from the oddest places that I'd miss if my mind weren't open and ready to take it in.

I'm also a voracious reader of magazines on subjects from technology to fashion. Good magazines are a source

Product: Exclamation Pen!
Designer: Joel Delman
Company: Twenty Twenty Thinking
Client: Traffic Works, Inc.
Year: 1999
Photo: Joel Delman

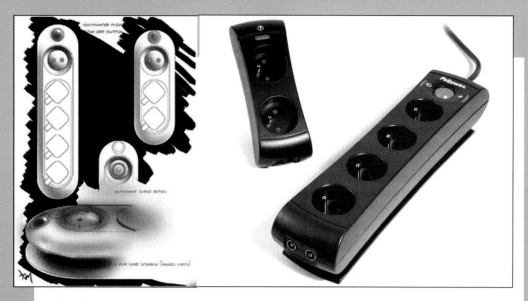

Product: Eurosurge Surge
Protectors
Designers: Joel Delman, Tim
Morton, Donna Piacenza, Clifford
Krapfle
Company: Product Development
Technologies, Inc.
Client: Fellowes, Inc.
Year: 2002
Photo: Tanya Sillitti

of inspiration and a knowledge base for what's out there, what's
not, and opportunities I can capitalize on as a designer. I also
read the *Wall Street Journal* every day cover to cover. Design is a
business, and what designers do is very much a part of the world
of dollars and cents. I need to understand that not only for the
way it directly impacts my work but to speak intelligently with
clients and understand their needs in the context of the business
environment they compete in.

**When you are designing, who finally says "this is it"? The
client? You?**
The client has the final say most of the time, but if I've done my
job well, I've managed to lead them through a series of decisions
to a final solution that I would have picked myself. A good rule of
thumb to keep in mind: Never present something to a client that
you don't want them to select because invariably that's the one
they'll pick if you give them the chance.

Do you do a lot of research? Focus groups?
My firm views research as an indispensable key to quality design
solutions, and we encourage clients to support design research on
every project where time and budget permit. Direct observation of
people using products, involving them in the research process,
provides far more insight than focus groups into users' needs and
ways to address them.

When you are designing, how do you work? Do you mock things up in your shop?
From two-dimensional pencil sketching to three-dimensional computer geometry, today's designer has a fantastic array of tools to work with. Judicious use of them all—that means careful use of the computer, particularly at the early stages of concept development—allows our team to approach problems from a variety of angles before converging on final solutions.

As a general observation, I can always tell when a product has been designed on the computer. Form development is the heart of any aesthetic statement, and there is simply no substitute for carving lots of foam to gain a real understanding of how a product will look and feel from all angles.

Hand-carving foam models to develop 3D form

Is designing fun? Why?
It's one of the only things a person can do that truly shapes the world. There's an incredible kick to seeing a product start as a napkin scribble and develop into something on the shelf at Target.

What's in your future? What do you want to design?
Lots more toys. There's no more challenging category of product to work in, no more demanding end user to please.

Who are your clients?
We work with a variety of manufacturers, providing design and engineering services for everything from consumer electronics to recreational vehicles to medical equipment. PDT designs more mobile phones than any other firm in the United States and is generally known for hand-held products.

How do you work? In collaboration? Alone?
Always with others. Even the smallest project demands the synergy that two good minds can provide.

Can you sum up your design philosophy in one word? Why?
Simplify. Dieter Rams once said that "good design means as little design as possible," and I couldn't agree more. The best designs invariably use the fewest elements needed to create a cohesive, meaningful aesthetic statement that's closely in tune with the way the product works.

Synergen (That Which Produces Synergy)

DESIGNER: TREVOR COMBS

Title: Founder
Firm Name: Super Innovative Concepts, Inc.
Location: Gaithersburg, Maryland

How did you discover industrial design?
By doing it! I designed a problem-solving product for personal use and met an industrial designer in the process of trying to sell my design. I never knew that anyone but engineers did this stuff.

How do you work?
Great design does not happen in a vacuum! I try to share with as many people as possible and process their feedback. I try to do this up front because much time can be wasted under the assumption that I know it all.

Actual form epiphany happens at any time, so I try to always be ready to whip out a quick sketch to help me retain the idea until I can get time to work on it. Soon as possible, I go into three dimensions with a wood or foam model. Taking an unadvisable amount of shortcuts, I feel my way to a design that works enough to be a starting point for CAD. I work with a couple of really talented engineers, who with three-dimensional scanning and tremendous skill recreate my model in CAD; it can then be manipulated, corrected, sized, and so on. Finite Element Analysis (FEA) is run on the structural parts; results are used for design

Product: Phly-by Handlebar Ends
Designer: Trevor Combs
Creative Director: Trevor Combs
Year: In development
Photo: Bronwen Sexton

Product: Slam X-12
Magnesium Handlebar Stem
Designers: Trevor Combs,
Jack Witmer
Creative Director: Trevor
Combs
Year: 2001
Photos: Trevor Combs

changes and location of the
strain gauges that will be
used for destructive testing.
I do none of the CAD work myself! The products are not
hindered by my inability to work a computer or shop tool.

**Designing consumer products must be a challenge, given the
high volumes and design constraints.**
Creating structural and performance bike parts is a huge
challenge. If I get it wrong, people could be seriously injured,
paralyzed, or even die! Conversely, if certain parts are 35 grams
overweight, they might not sell. The bike industry is odd in
that we need really sophisticated stuff, but volumes are
laughably low.

Where do you get your ideas?
I try to find ideas from something seemingly unrelated and
extrapolate its essence to arrive at new and fresh ideas. That's a
good way to avoid sophomoric design statements.

**When you are designing, who finally says, "this is it"? The
client? You?**
Nearly every time I make a new iteration of a design I think, "This
is it!" Thank God I don't deal with clients anymore. My experience
is that most make the wrong choice most of the time. In the end,
the market tells us what is hot and what is not.

I functioned as a hack interior designer for the offices that
house our family-owned businesses. I really struggled with the
layout and real doubts about how the place was going to look,
feel, and function. To make a long story short, the regional
president of our bank wants to give me design reign over a
building they're putting up nearby!

Product: Slam X-24 Magnesium
Handlebar Stem
Designers: Trevor Combs, Jack
Witmer
Creative Director: Trevor
Combs
Year: 2001
Photo: Trevor Combs

Do you do a lot of research? Focus groups?

Yes! I am constantly doing research in that I'm canvassing everything all the time: new products, materials, color palettes, whatever. I read every issue of four cycling magazines, go to races, try new parts by other manufacturers. I subscribe to technical and manufacturing magazines to stay up on new materials and processes. I go to fashion shows, movies, and architectural exhibits to see where trends are going.

I'm not big on focus groups because I don't believe people can tell you what they're looking for. When we do a show, I watch body language and notice what kinds of comments and questions come up.

When you are designing, how do you work? Do you mock things up in your shop?

I draw life-size or bigger on rolls of brown Kraft paper in the beginning. I'm just trying to draw a nice picture and play with any curves and movements that might be there. Using big, fat pastels and broad markers helps keep it quick and spontaneous. As soon as possible, I jump into three dimensions so I can really see what I've got. I prefer to use a material that's as soft and cheap as possible at first (to take away things that add time and anal retentiveness). I make a series, with each one building on what I've learned from making the last. I make as few as four and as many as I have to.

After I have a form I like, the last thing I do is use the band saw, drill press, and grinders (machines, not hand-held tools) to see if I can perform steps tool operators at a factory might actually perform to make this piece. Generally I find that if I can clamp the thing down and make this thing given my rudimentary tools, the form is manufacturable for a decent price.

When I have a final form that is at least a starting point, I either finish it for show or, if we're on the fast track, send it right to engineering for 3D scanning. After that, success depends on my ability to articulate changes by e-mail, phone, fax, digital picture swapping, and envisioning a desirable finishing for the product.

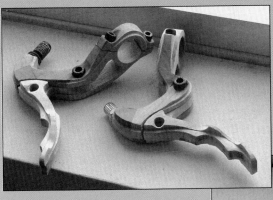

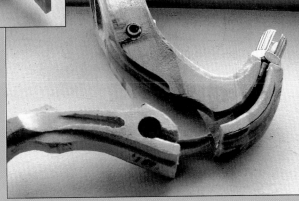

Product: Wood mockups of Five-O
Brake Levers
Designer: Trevor Combs
Year: In development
Photos: Trevor Combs

Is designing fun? Why?

Designing is the most awesome activity on the planet! Feelings of accomplishment, stimulation of intellectual challenge, thrill of the gamble, and opportunity for self-expression are things we try to capture in many activities. A bonus is that the stuff I design is used for fun, so I can theoretically make more fun in the process.

Do you have a few words of wisdom for people starting their own design business?

Write a business plan! Reread and adjust it every six months. Get more than one partner with a long-range mentality and skill sets that do not overlap with your own. Preferably, one partner has a client list and the other actually enjoys business administration. Be sure that everyone working for you is actually smarter and sharper than you are!

Can you sum up your design philosophy in one word? Why?

Synergen (that which produces synergy). Design is about the successful integration of concepts, form, function, price points, production methods, and so on. Integrating all these concerns into a salable package is the role of the designer. I would say the successful product represents a synergy of concerns.

Experience

DESIGNER: ANDRÉ GRASSO

Title: Principal
Firm Name: Index Industrial Design and
Development
Location: Garrison, New York

How do you work? How do you attack a design problem?
One analogy we use to describe the design process is a simple
line: at one end, the proverbial sketch on a napkin and, at the
other, the finished product in the box. What is critical to the
success of this process and products you design is the knowledge
you have while guiding your clients and navigating this line.

   We approach each project with the same vigor, concerns, and
consideration, whether we are designing heavy-duty products,
tools, construction equipment, medical products, architectural
products, or safety and emergency products. Usually a clear
problem has to be solved, although
it is constrained by engineering,
regulatory, safety, or ergonomic
requirements. Even though every
product and project differs, we beg
clients to let us do it our way to get
them to the one best solution for
their product.

**Tell me about A-La-Cart for Hertz.
How did the design happen? How
do you go about building cars?**
That was a clean-sheet-of-paper
project. The idea was to create a
vehicle that would almost literally
take the counter to a customer in a
facility parking lot. In large Hertz
locations, either on their own

Product: Concrete Vibrator
Designers: Doug Winer, Ryan Shafer,
Shaw Zu, Robert Kleinschmidt
Creative Director: André Grasso
Client: Stow/Bomag Light
Equipment Division
Year: 1999

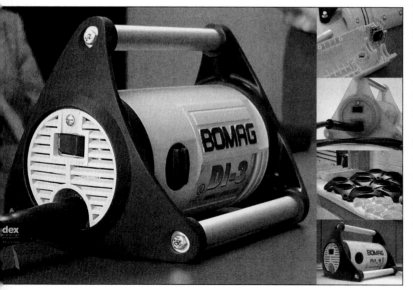

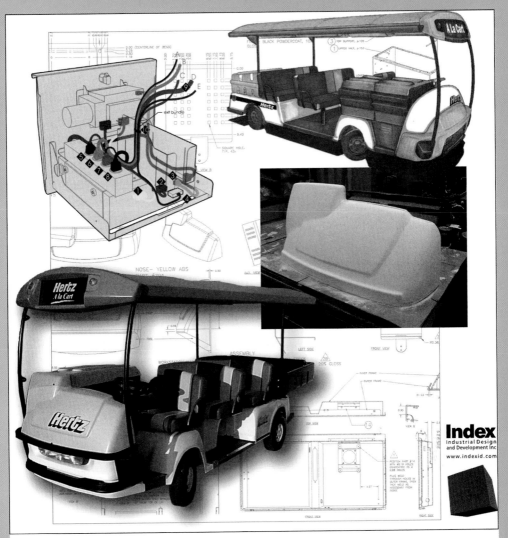

properties or at airports, customers traverse large parking lots to locate their rental car, and sometimes there is a need to change cars. So rather than have customers return to the rental counter to make changes, Hertz wanted the ability to revise or change rental agreements out in the lot and deliver the customer to the new rental vehicle. The need was to produce an economical vehicle suitable for sheltered transportation of four to six customers and their luggage that housed a wireless workstation containing all equipment necessary for a rental transaction.

Product: Hertz A-La-Cart
Designers: Joel Miller, Shaw Zu, Robert Kleinschmidt
Creative Director: André Grasso
Client: Hertz Corporation
Year: 1999

We designed this product the same way we approach other products. Initially we conducted a concept phase to investigate vehicle platforms, component configurations, features, safety and technical requirements, and the like. Once we had defined the concept, we immediately launched into producing a full-sized mockup of the proposed vehicle. The final vehicle platform was based on an electric golf cart that provided instant frame, suspension, and power train. Components that required tooling were produced with foam materials; some components had to be fabricated from metal materials for structure or simplicity; and the workstation was fabricated from wood and plastic materials. The finished mockup was more of a working model. The vehicle was drivable, the workstation was online, and all other features were represented and functioning.

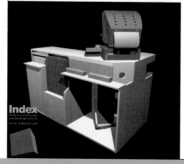

Product: Hertz Workstation
Designers: André Grasso, Joel Miller
Creative Director: André Grasso
Client: Hertz Corporation
Year: 2000

Once we were given the nod by Hertz, we had to design, detail, and document every component and piece of hardware and hope it all fit together. With all development documentation completed, the next step was to produce two prototypes of the vehicle for beta testing at specific locations. Index produced and assembled both the mockup and prototypes at our facility. Finally, we were asked to produce and build twenty-seven vehicles. Based on the prototype experience, we made necessary revisions to our documents and issued a production document package, tweaked the tooling, produced product and maintenance manuals to accompany the vehicle, and proceeded to build twenty-seven vehicles and ship them to Hertz locations around the country.

You also design other stuff for Hertz. What is it and why?
We have been designing an enormous variety of stuff for Hertz since 1984. Hertz, being a service company, is kind of an odd client for a product design firm, but they use products to sell or support their service, programs, and facilities.

Some of the things we have designed have been unique: counters and workstations, the Return Center, A-La-Cart, thermal printer enclosures, Return Vaults, Kiosks, Signature Capture Units, Gold Program Signage. In the past year and a half we have been designing and developing forty to fifty new standard signage products to support services and programs and for traffic management and wayfinding.

Product: Integrated Helmet
Designers: John Laverk, Doug Winer, Mark Pug
Creative Director: André Grasso
Client: Mine Safety Appliances
Year: 1993

How do you test your designs? Do you make a lot of prototypes?
Not enough, as far as I'm concerned. One of the most difficult parts of designing products is to get clients to understand the need and value in producing not just one prototype or three-dimensional representation of the product being designed. One day I got tired of constantly correcting and explaining to clients about the word

prototype. So I created a glossary for our clients that defined all the things we do to differentiate between mockups, appearance models, and ultimately and finally a prototype. We usually have to battle to produce every type of three-dimensional representation of the product we are developing to evaluate decisions we are making. Even though we use our engineering software to mechanize and move assemblies and products in real time, I usually don't believe it until we build something. There's just nothing like some stuff bolted together in front of you to make you see what has to be done to make it work.

You not only design, you manufacture. How does that work?
It started with a few clients and projects that we worked right through to the end of the design line, which left us with production documents and prototypes in hand and the client needing product. Often the products were lower-volume, hundreds to under 2,000 items. It's a win-win situation for clients. Rather than us dumping a load of drawings and CAD files on the client's engineering department, we have the guys who designed the thing for nine to fourteen months deal with it.

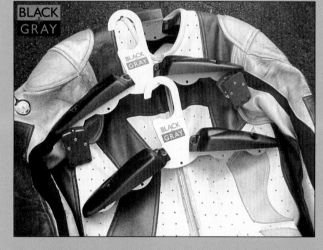

Product: Hi-Per Hanger
Designer: Joel Miller
Creative Director: André Grasso
Client: BLACK+GRAY
Design+Manufacturing, Inc.
Year: 2002

For us it does a couple of things. Aside from the additional business it generates for Index and added benefits for clients, it puts us way down at the end of the design line, and these experiences make for good product designers. It is also a efficient process. Index understands the product, we know the best source for processes and components, we have established relationships with suppliers, we understand and can judge what is acceptable from suppliers, and when something is wrong we know how to fix it.

Can you sum up your design philosophy in one word?
Experience. That doesn't seem profound, but I think, unlike other professions, the more experience and experiences product designers have, the better their chances are of being good product designers.

Faith

DESIGNER: DOUG GREEN

Title: Founder and Designer
Firm Name: Green Design Furniture
Location: Portland, Maine

Why did you start your own company?
Frustration and innocence. After spending three years developing a promising process for manufacturing furniture, I finally finished the patent application process and dragged prototypes to demonstrations for prominent furniture manufacturers, but I couldn't find a willing buyer. Green Design Furniture Co. was incorporated in 1993 to become the first manufacturer to use my patented process and to begin the revolution in furniture making. I sometimes compare my experience with that of becoming a parent. Giving birth to an invention is the easy part. Then your life revolves around finding ways to nurture the idea and provide a safe environment for it to grow and thrive. You follow where it wants to go and try to figure out what it wants and needs.

Product: Classic File Credenza
Designer: Doug Green
Description: The reverse tapered leg and bevel-edged top are a signature of Green Design Furniture's earlier designs. Two file drawers hold legal or letter-size hanging folders and two smaller drawers add utility.

How did you come up with the idea that started the company?
I needed a sofa for my studio apartment, As I began sketching my perfect sofa, I became intrigued with its most basic elements. One of the early drawings shows long sliding dovetails on the ends of the seat and back that create the sofa's structure. I realized I had stumbled upon something. Within a month I had shop drawings for several prototypes, each assembled in a specific sequence with self-locking dovetail joints. I began prototyping at a friend's shop in Maine. The long sliding dovetails were difficult to make and required much tinkering. It

Green Design Furniture uses an original patented process of interlocking joinery that virtually eliminated the use of screws, nuts, bolts, and other fasteners. Full-length dovetails slide smoothly into place. This self-locking joinery allows for the seasonal movement of the wood without warping, distortion, or loosening.

wasn't until the second prototype chair was finished that I had the eureka moment. A year later, I had prototyped fifteen different pieces of furniture using variations of that first idea.

How do you work?

The first phase of my design process is the longest and takes the most discipline. Concept drawings are quickly rendered and usually show the progression of a solution, incremental changes, journeys down avenues that don't work. I do not begin prototyping until I feel confident I have a resolved idea. The next step is translating the idea into working shop drawings using a three-dimensional computer design program called Graphite on a Macintosh platform. I use the same program to design the manufacturing jigs and templates I need to fabricate the parts.

Prototyping in our woodworking shop is one of the most enjoyable activities I can imagine. Bringing the concept into three dimensions provides more opportunities for discovery and invention. Refining proportions and discovering new ideas for construction are a natural part of this hands-on process. It is also another arena for experimentation and fortuitous accident. While working on the first Series 2 designs, I had made extra tops to see how different treatments of a curved edge would look on the table. None of the versions I had come up with were working. In the middle of sanding off a curved edge that had a bevel cut underneath, I happened to look at the edge and discovered I had inadvertently created an unusual pattern in which the thickness of the top seemed to decrease toward the middle. Within an hour, I had figured out a series of cuts that created a beautiful curve on the underside of the edge. This happy accident gave me the visual key that was to become the unifying theme of our Series 2 pieces.

Another wonderful aspect of prototyping is that it is the most public part of our design process. Opinions are plentiful in the shop and often result in improvements. Finished prototypes are then displayed in our retail showroom, where more opinions are solicited. Typically a new piece goes through two or three revisions in prototype stage until it is ready to be photographed for our next catalog.

Product: Bedroom suite
Designer: Doug Green

The great luxury of owning my own company is that my designs are an expression of my personal vision for how furniture should be made and how it should look and function. I spend a great deal of time listening to our customers and researching their needs and desires.

What's in your future? What do you want to design?

I aspire to see my assembly system, which I call "craftsman programming," become an industry standard. It demonstrates that it's possible to use the most sophisticated technology to make something that is simple, strong, and of lasting beauty. I dream of creating a design factory where our product would be innovative ideas for improving a variety of manufactured objects. I want to continue working on ideas that challenge conventional ways of doing things that are wasteful, inefficient, or just plain dumb.

Do you have a few words of wisdom for people starting their own design business?

Building a successful business is a creative and demanding undertaking. The painful truth is that the greatest threat to the success of an entrepreneurial business is the entrepreneur

Product: Classic Armchair and
Classic Ottoman
Designer: Doug Green

himself. Managing a successful,
growing business requires a whole
different set of skills and interests,
which the entrepreneur can learn or
delegate. If possible, use someone
else's money even if you don't have
to. You'll learn better discipline
much faster if you're accountable to
someone who is writing the checks.

If you want to retain control over
the quality of the products you
create, then you're a spoiled brat
like me who really wants to be his
own client. I spend most of my waking hours managing the
growth of my business, so I'm happy when I get a few precious
hours for designing. The thing I love about owning a design
business is that I am able to measure the success or failure of an
idea directly from our customers, who let me know on a daily
basis how I'm doing. I can work on a design until I get it right,
and then I can keep improving it.

Can you sum up your design philosophy in one word? Why?
Faith. You must have faith to believe something is possible when
you can't know it exists. If I didn't have faith that the truthful
idea was out there, I would never have the courage to set out on
the design process. Because I have faith, I can endure all the
wrong ideas, false starts, and dead ends that must be encountered
along the way. Faith allows me to enjoy the process and to
understand that the journey is the purpose of my life.

Product: Home office suite
Designer: Doug Green
Company: Green Design Furniture

Portfolio

Sitting in the corridor outside Dean Albert Christ-Janner's office at Pratt was terrifying. I had begun to believe going to art school was a possibility! But when I arrived with my brown paper bag full of sketches and watercolors, I was sure I wouldn't be accepted. Everyone else had a portfolio: I couldn't even spell it, much less did I know that such things existed. They looked at my work and didn't even comment on my brown bag portfolio. To this day I don't have a portfolio. And take all my work and models to clients in plastic garbage bags (just a little flashier than brown paper bags). They also make it easy to dispose of rejected ideas! I leaned that people judge the work, not what it is wrapped in.

—Excerpted from "Turning Points," *Innovation* (Winter 1992), published by the IDSA

Presentation

Presentation isn't everything, but it does count for something. When putting together a portfolio, think about what's in it first, not what the format is. Be straightforward and honest in your presentation of the ideas. Glitter looks good at first, but content is what people eventually get to—and if isn't there, well, it just isn't there. Designers look at portfolios in a detached way. They are judging the work and, by extension, you. In some ways it's a beauty contest.

Skills

A portfolio should show your strengths. What do you do well? Portfolios demonstrate the work you have done, how you achieved it, where you did it, and who your collaborators were—clearly! Portfolios for product design vary from specialty to specialty, but everyone is looking for the basic skills: drawing, sketching, model making, and communication. Computer skills are at the top of everyone's list, so learn a few three-dimensional drawing programs—maybe Solidworks, Pro-E, Vellum, and surface model and rendering programs like Alias and two-dimensional programs like Adobe PhotoShop. Build something with your computer skills. Show how you think. In the end, though, everyone communicates initially with simple sketches done on regular letter-sized paper. Your portfolio should demonstrate how well you sketch quick, clear ideas.

Process

A portfolio should show your understanding of design processes, starting with sketches and moving to quick three-dimensional sketches. It should show how these sketches, both two-dimensional and three-dimensional, were tested and criticized by your teachers or, better yet, by real people and how the criticism and testing altered the design. A pretty model of a telephone doesn't cut it if it hasn't been properly tested or criticized. If you are looking for a job in the automotive industry, drawings of automobiles are a must, but demonstrating an understanding of how the auto industry designs may be more important. Showing through your work that you understand their design process will help in at least getting an interview.

Point of View

Build your portfolio based on your point of view—what you think is important in design. Where you stand on issues will also help you decide the sort of place you want to work. If you are interested in issues such as ecology or green design or universal design, make that clear in your portfolio. In most instances, your point of view is what you will be judged on next, after skills.

Communication

How you use your skills is important. How you think using skills is also important. Product designers must communicate their ideas clearly and rapidly. As a product designer, you not only come up with ideas but also must get them across to other designers, engineers, manufacturers, and marketers. Designing the product is the easy part; communicating your idea to others is the hard part. All these professionals speak slightly different languages and have different agendas. Understanding and demonstrating that you can communicate with various types of people in your portfolio will help you. Showing the progress of a product from conception to reality convinces potential employers you are ready to become a product designer.

Internships

Frankly, interns often do the lousy jobs, like going for coffee and sweeping up the shop. But an internship is a great opportunity to test out a design specialty or design shop to see if it is where you belong. Internships at some design studios are much better than I just described. Some studios allow interns to design. To get your feet wet, test the waters. As a student in the Fashion Institute of Technology Toy Design Program you must do an internship in toy design as part of your school experience; in fact, many design schools now require an internship prior to graduation.

Testing Skills

An internship allows you to test your skills and to find out what you need to improve on or learn. It's a great way to find out how design is done professionally. Professional designers work at a much more rapid pace then most schools. They rarely have the luxury of time to contemplate a design over and over. I think most interns are astonished at how quickly a design is accomplished. Adapting to the rapid pace of a design office is probably the most difficult part of the experience.

Location, Location, Location

Where you choose to do an internship can color your ideas about product design. Again, you are trying to find out where you fit. Doing more than one internship is a good idea—ideally, one in a small design office and another in a manufacturing facility. The two offer quite different design experiences. A manufacturing facility has a stringent set of manufacturing capabilities and methods, and you will design to the manufacturer's strengths. If they make rotationally molded outdoor play equipment, most likely you will be designing outdoor play equipment. At a small design firm, your experience may vary from medical equipment to graphics to consumer products. So doing more than one internship can give you a clearer understanding of the type of design experience that is right for you.

Team Player

An internship may be your initiation into the world of team design. Teams, made up of designers, marketers, engineers, and manufacturing people, do most product design. This is only an example; teams can have any number of specialists on them, from biologists to economists. Designing isn't the solo experience it used to be. Being a good team player is important. It's a skill best learned playing on different teams, and it's one of the skills you develop during your internship.

Finding a Match

There are all kinds of internships. Some are paying while others are for credit. Most schools provide counseling for internship placement. Finding a perfect match can be difficult because there is a lot of competition for internships. Most manufacturing companies that employ designers, as in the automotive industry, offer internships, but they are highly competitive and require interviews and portfolio presentations. Start looking for an internship the day you feel confident enough to think you can design something or want to learn more about design. This may occur while you are in high school or later. Davin Stowell of Smart Design started working at the Corning Design Center while he was still in high school. He knew he wanted to be a product designer that early. For most of you, it may not be that early—but the sooner you start experiencing the real world of design, the better choices you will make. Design firms both small and large are looking for interns. It is a way for them to introduce young designers to the design experience.

Counseling

Most schools employ internship coordinators who provide you with specific information on how their programs operate. School policy may dictate whether internships are for credit or for pay. Most internships for credit require a site supervisor to oversee your work and present an evaluation of it at both midterm and the end of the internship. Some schools require that learning contracts be signed by both the student and the site supervisor. The contract outlines the student's duties and how the evaluations will be made. The contract ensures both the student and employer of a fair and productive internship.

Industry-Funded Projects

Some schools cultivate industry-funded projects that provide similar experiences to internships. Pratt Institute's SPAN is a not-for-profit organization that provides internships for students right on the Pratt campus. SPAN works on projects that range from products to environments to graphics.

"Who Are Your Heroes?"

Isamu Noguchi, who created beautiful objects that connect object with nature, crossing boundaries between Eastern and Western culture and bringing a timeless quality to our man-made environment.
—Eric Chan, ECCO Design

Ingo Maurer. As far as the lighting design world goes, he is a god. And his work is beautiful. Every time I go into his store my breath is taken away.
—Alecia Wesner, George Kovacs Lighting

Julia Child and Leonardo da Vinci.
—Debera Johnson, Pratt Institute

Donald Dohner, who started the design program at Carnegie Institute of Technology in 1934 and at Pratt Institute in 1935. The curriculum he created is still in use in most design schools. His view of design was broad in that he included human factors, materials and processes, and marketing. He also recognized the importance of women in the marketplace.
—Jim Lesko, University of Bridgeport

The designers George Nelson and Henry Dreyfuss and the sculptors Donald Judd and Isamu Noguchi.
—Harry Allen, Harry Allen Design, Inc.

My mom and the sculptor Andy Goldsworthy.
—Leslie Muller, Ray-Ban, A Luxottica Group Company

George Nelson, in terms of his design and vision. George Carlin, the comedian, because he talks about the stuff and things around us. Sybil Moholy Nagy, author of *Matrix and Man*, who gave me a vision of where design is in a historical context.
—Fred Blumlein, Blumlein Associates, Inc.

Victor Papanek, because he was one of the first designers to think green.
—Wendy E. Brawer, Green Map System and Modern World

Gene Kelley, the Beatles, Alexander Calder. They exemplify to me the idea that work and fun can be one and the same. I love that they were successful and happy, and their work was a pure expression of that joy. I also love the work of Isamu Noguchi, although I don't know whether he was a happy fellow. I idolize Frank Lloyd Wright for his genius, his fabulous self-confidence, and his amazingly prolific and inventive imagination.
—Doug Green, Green Design Furniture

I don't really have a hero. I have a teacher who taught me self-knowledge, which is a practical way to feel the contentment already within each one of us. As a result, everyday living has become more enjoyable.
—Mario Turchi, Ion Design

Charles Eames. The brilliance of his work is well known. I met him once and I was overwhelmed by his modesty and shyness and overpowered by his creativity and commitment to design. He shared some history of the design of his famous home and his oft-quoted belief that good design requires constraints. On the arrival at the site of all the premanufactured components of the house, Ray and Charles Eames challenged themselves to completely redesign the house using only the components on site—no more, no less. The result of that constraint is a house that is now a museum.
—Steve Thurston, University of Idaho

Pierre Chareau, Edward Wormley.
—Ron Kemnitzer, Kemnitzer Design

Schools Offering Degrees in Product Design

Academy of Art College
Product and Industrial Design Department
79 New Montgomery Street
San Francisco, California 94105
Phone: 415-749-2611
Fax: 415-749-2610
Degrees: BFA, MFA

Arizona State University
College of Architecture
School of Design
Tempe, Arizona 85287-2105
Phone: 480-965-4135
Fax: 480-965-9717
Degrees: BS, MS, PhD

Art Center College of Design
1700 Lida Street, Box 7197
Pasadena, California
91103-7197
Phone: 626-396-2200
Fax: 626-795-0819
Degree: BS, MS

Art Institute of Colorado
1200 Lincoln
Denver, Colorado 80203
Phone: 303-860-8520
Fax: 303-764-9755
Degree: BA

Art Institute of Fort Lauderdale
1799 SE 17th Street
Fort Lauderdale, Florida
33316-3000
Phone: 954-463-3000
Fax: 954-523-7676
Degree: BS

Art Institute of Philadelphia
1622 Chestnut Street
Philadelphia, PA 19103-5198
Phone: 215-567-7080
Fax: 215-405-6399
Degree: BS

Art Institute of Pittsburgh
420 Boulevard of The Allies
Pittsburgh, PA 15219
Phone: 800-275-2470
Fax: 412-263-6667
Degree: AS/BS

Art Institute of Seattle
2323 Elliott Avenue
Seattle, WA 98121
Phone: 206-448-0900
Fax: 206-269-0275
Degree: AAA

Auburn University
Department of Industrial Design
207 Wallace Center
Auburn, Alabama 36849-5121
Phone: 334-844-2364
Fax: 334-844-2367
Degree: BID, MID

Brigham Young University
P.O. Box 24206
Provo, Utah 84602-4206
Phone: 801-378-4880
Fax: 801-378-2954
Degree: BFA

California College of Arts and Crafts
1111 8th Street
San Francisco, California 94107
Phone: 415-703-9500
Fax: 415-621-2396
Degrees: BFA, MFA

California State University, Long Beach
Department of Design
1250 Bellflower Boulevard
Long Beach, CA 90840-3401
Phone: 562-985-5089
Fax: 562-985-2284
Degrees: BS, MA

California State University, Northridge
Art Department
18111 Nordhoff Street
Northridge, California
91330-8300
Phone: 818-677-2242
Fax: 818-677-3046
Degree: BA

Carnegie Mellon University
School of Design
110 Margaret Morrison
Pittsburgh, Pennsylvania
15213-3890
Phone: 412-268-2828
Fax: 412-268-3088
Degrees: BFA, MDes

Cleveland Institute of Art
11141 East Boulevard
Cleveland, Ohio 44106
Phone: 216-421-7000
Fax: 216-421-7438
Degree: BFA

College for Creative Studies
201 East Kirby Street
Detroit, Michigan 48202-4034
Phone: 313-664-7630
Fax: 313-873-4010
Degree: BFA

Columbus College of Art and Design
107 North Ninth Street
Columbus, Ohio 43215-1758
Phone: 614-224-9101
Fax: 614-222-4040
Degree: BFA

Cranbrook Academy of Art
Department of Industrial
Design
39221 North Woodward Avenue
Bloomfield Hills, Michigan
48303-0801
Phone: 248-645-3300
Fax: 248-646-0046
Degree: MFA

Georgia Institute of Technology
School of Architecture
Industrial Design Program
247 Fourth Street NW
Atlanta, Georgia 30332-0155
Phone: 404-894-4874
Fax: 404-894-3396
Degrees: BS, MS

Illinois Institute of Technology
Institute of Design
350 North LaSalle Street
Chicago, Illinois 60610
Phone: 312-595-4900
Fax: 312-595-4901
Degrees: MDes, MDM, PhD

ITT Technical Institute
630 East Brier Drive, Suite 150
San Bernardino, California
92408
Phone: 909-889-3800
Fax: 909-888-6970
Degrees: BAS, MS

ITT Technical Institute
4919 Coldwater Road
Fort Wayne, Indiana
46825-5532
Phone: 219-484-4107
Fax: 219-484-0860
Degree: BAS

ITT Technical Institute
920 West Levoy Drive
Murray, Utah 84123
Phone: 801-263-3313
Fax: 801-263-3497
Degree: BAS

Kendall College of Art and Design
111 North Division Avenue
Grand Rapids, Michigan
49503-3102
Phone: 800-676-2787
Fax: 616-451-9867
Degree: BFA

Massachusetts College of Art
621 Huntington Avenue
Boston, Massachusetts
02115-5882
Phone: 617-879-7650
Fax: 617-566-5374
Degrees: BFA, MFA

Metropolitan State College
Campus Box 90
P.O. Box 173362
Denver, Colorado 80217-3362
Phone: 303-556-3219
Fax: 303-556-3656
Degree: BA

Milwaukee Institute of Art and Design
273 East Erie Street
Milwaukee, Wisconsin
53202-6003
Phone: 414-276-7889
Fax: 414-291-8077
Degree: BFA

North Carolina State University
School of Design
Box 7701
Raleigh, North Carolina
27695-7701
Phone: 919-515-8322
Fax: 919-515-7330
Degrees: BID, MID

The Ohio State University
Room 380, Hopkins Hall
128 North Oval Mall
Columbus, Ohio 43210
Phone: 614-292-6746
Fax: 614-292-0217
Degrees: BS, MA

Parsons School of Design
66 Fifth Avenue
New York, New York 10011
Phone: 212-229-5885
Fax: 212-229-5374
Degree: BFA

Philadelphia University
Industrial Design/Smith House
Schoolhouse Lane and Henry
Avenue
Philadelphia, Pennsylvania
19144-5497
Phone: 215-951-2109
Fax: 215-951-6865
Degree: BS

Pratt Institute
200 Willoughby Avenue
Industrial Design Department
Brooklyn, New York 11205
Phone: 718-636-3631
Fax: 718-636-3553
Degrees: BID, MID

Purdue University
Division of Art and Design
1352 Creative Arts Building #1
West Lafayette, Indiana 47907
Phone: 765-494-2295
Fax: 765-496-1198
Degrees: BA, MA, IDE

Rhode Island School of Design
2 College Street
Providence, Rhode Island
02903-2784
Phone: 401-454-6160
Fax: 401-232-2503
Degrees: BFA, BID, MID

Rochester Institute of Technology
CIAS/School of Design
Department of Industrial
Design
73 Lomb Memorial Drive
Rochester, New York
14623-5603
Phone: 716-475-2668
Fax: 716-475-7533
Degrees: BFA, MFA

San Francisco State University
Department of Design
1600 Holloway
San Francisco, California
94132-1740
Phone: 415-338-2229
Fax: 415-338-7770
Degrees: BA, MA

San Jose State University
School of Art and Design
One Washington Square
San Jose, California
95192-0089
Phone: 408-924-4343
Fax: 408-924-4326
Degree: BS

Savannah College of Art and Design
P.O. Box 3146
Savannah, Georgia 31402-3146
Phone: 912-525-6430
Fax: 912-525-6427
Degrees: BFA, MFA, MA

Southern Illinois University
School of Art and Design
Mail Code 4301
Carbondale, Illinois 62901
Phone: 618-453-4313
Fax: 618-453-7710
Degrees: BA, BFA

Stanford University
Design Department, School of
Art
Design Division, Terman 551
Stanford, California
94305-4021
Phone: 650-723-4288
Fax: 650-723-3521
Degrees: BS, MS, MFA

Syracuse University
334 Smith Hall
Syracuse, New York 13244-0001
Phone: 315-443-9691
Fax: 315-443-9688
Degrees: BID, MID

The University of the Arts
Industrial Design Department
4th Floor, Anderson Hall
320 South Broad Street
Philadelphia, Pennsylvania
19102-4901
Phone: 215-717-6250
Fax: 215-717-6255
Degrees: BS, MID

University of Bridgeport
Department of Industrial
Design
600 University Avenue
Bridgeport, Connecticut
06601-2449
Phone: 203-576-4222
Fax: 203-576-4051
Degree: BS

University of Cincinnati
Department of Industrial
Design
P.O. Box 210016
Cincinnati, Ohio 45221-0016
Phone: 513-556-6828
Fax: 513-556-0240
Degrees: BS, MDes

University of Illinois, Chicago
929 West Harrison
106 Jefferson Hall, M/C036
Chicago, Illinois 60607-7038
Phone: 312-996-3337
Fax: 312-413-2333
Degrees: BFA, MFA

**University of Illinois,
Urbana-Champaign**
School of Art and Design
408 East Peabody Drive
Champaign, Illinois 61820
Phone: 217-333-0855
Fax: 217-244-7688
Degrees: BFA, MFA

University of Kansas
Art and Design Building #300
1467 Jayhawk Boulevard
Lawrence, Kansas 66045
Phone: 785-864-4401
Fax: 785-864-4404
Degrees: BFA, MFA

University of Michigan
2000 Bonisteel Boulevard
Ann Arbor, Michigan
48109-2069
Phone: 734-764-0397
Fax: 734-936-0469
Degrees: BFA, MFA

University of Notre Dame
32 O'Shaughnessy Hall
Department of Art, Art History,
and Design
Notre Dame, Indiana
46556-5639
Phone: 219-631-7602
Fax: 219-631-6312
Degrees: BA, BFA, MFA

University of Washington
School of Art
Box 353440
Seattle, Washington
98195-3440
Phone: 206-543-0970
Fax: 206-685-1657
Degrees: BFA, MFA

**University of Wisconsin,
Stout**
Department of Art and Design
Applied Arts Building
Menomonie, Wisconsin
54751-0790
Phone: 715-232-1097
Fax: 715-232-1669
Degree: BFA

Virginia Polytechnic Institute
Industrial Design Program
202 Cowgill Hall
Blacksburg, Virginia
24061-0205
Phone: 540-231-6386
Fax: 540-231-6332
Degrees: BS, MS

**Wentworth Institute of
Technology**
Department of Design and
Facilities
550 Huntington Avenue
Boston, Massachusetts
02115-5901
Phone: 617-989-4050
Fax: 617-989-4172
Degree: BS

Western Michigan University
Department of Industrial
Design
1903 West Michigan Avenue
Kalamazoo, Michigan
49008-5316
Phone: 269-387-6515
Fax: 269-387-6517
Degree: BS

**Western Washington
University**
Department of Technology
516 High Street ET204
Bellingham, Washington 98225
Phone: 360-650-3425
Fax: 360-650-4847
Degree: BS

Design Organizations

Adaptive Environments
374 Congress Street, Suite 301
Boston, Massachusetts 02110
Phone: 617-695-1225
www.adaptiveenvironments.org

Advanced Design Institute
99 Toyon Drive
Fairfax, California 94930
www.advanceddesign.org

American Center for Design
325 West Huron, Suite 711
Chicago, Illinois 60610
Phone: 312-787-2018
www.ac4d.org

American Institute of Architects
1735 New York Avenue NW
Washington, DC 20006
Phone: 800-AIA-3837
Fax: 202-626-7547
Email: infocentre@aia.org
www.aia.org

American Institute of Graphic Arts
164 Fifth Avenue
New York, New York 10010
Phone: 212-807-1990
Fax: 212-807-1799
www.aiga.org

American Society of Landscape Architects
636 Eye Street NW
Washington, DC 20001-3736
Phone: 202-898-2444
Fax: 202-898-1185
www.asla.org

Association of Professional Design Firms
601 108th Avenue NE, Suite 1906
Bellview, Washington 98004
Phone: 425-943-3825
www.apdf.org

Chartered Society of Designers
5 Bermondsey Exchange
179-181 Bermondsey Street
London SE1 3UW
United Kingdom
Phone: 020 7357 8088
Fax: 020 7407 9878
Email: csd@csd.org.uk
www.csd.org.uk

Corporate Design Foundation
20 Park Plaza, Suite 321
Boston, Massachusetts 02116-4303
Phone: 617-350-7097
Fax: 617-451-6355
Email: admin@cdf.org
www.cdf.org

The Design Council
34 Bow Street
London WC2E 7DL
United Kingdom
Phone: 44 020 7420 5200
Fax: 44 020 7420 5300
Email: info@designcouncil.org.uk
www.design-council.org.uk/design

Design Management Institute
29 Temple Place, 2nd Floor
Boston, Massachusetts 02111-1350
Phone: 617-338-6380
Fax: 617-338-6570
www.dmi.org

Green Design
02NYC
02-usa.org/NYC
02 Global Net
www.02-usa.org

Human Factors and Ergonomics Society
P.O. Box 1369
Santa Monica, California 90406
Phone: 310-394-1811

Industrial Design Society of America (IDSA)
45195 Business Court, Suite 250
Dulles, Virginia 20166-6717
Phone: 703-707-6000
www.idsa.org

International Council of Societies of Industrial Designers
ICSID Secretariat
Erottajankatu 11 A 18
01300 Helsinki
Finland
Phone: 358 9 696 22 90
Fax: 358 9 686 22 910
icsidsec@icsid.org
www.icsid.org

The International Interior Design Association
Headquarters
13-122 Merchandise Mart
Chicago, Illinois 60654-1104
Phone: 312-467-1950
Fax: 312-467-0779
www.iida.org

Product Development Management Association
17000 Commerce Parkway,
Suite C
Mount Laurel, New Jersey 08054
Phone: 800-232-5241
Fax: 856-439-0525
www.pdma.org

The Raymond Loewy Foundation
P.O. Box 6998
Chicago, Illinois 60680-6998
Phone: 312-642-7534
www.raymondloewyfoundation.com

Society of Environmental Graphic Design
1000 Vermont Avenue, Suite 400
Washington, DC 20005
Phone: 202-638-5555
Fax: 202-636-0891
www.segd.org

Universal Design
IDEA Center
Center for Inclusive Design and Environmental Access
SUNY Buffalo
Phone: 716-829-2133
idea@arch.buffalo.edu

Index of Designers

Allen, Harry, 54
Arkay-Leliever, Christian, P., 231
Barna, Peter, 9
Bevan, Victoria, 154
Birsel, Ayse, 136
Blumlein, Fred, 184
Brawer, Wendy, E., 221
Bressler, Peter, 93
Cafaro, John, 207
Celentano, Linda, 162
Chan, Eric, 125
Clem, Bill, 72
Combs, Trevor, 250
Delman, Joel, 246
Demenge, Sophie, 122
Dziersk, Mark, 111
Ellis, Judy, 13
Fenton, Timm, 147
Goetz, Mark, 119
Grasso, André, 254
Green, Doug, 259
Hennes, Tom, 189
Hixon, Kate, 179
Johnson, Debera, 18
Justice, Lorraine, 26
Kapec, Jeff, 64
Kemnitzer, Ron, 128
Khachatoorian, Haig, 42
Lesko, Jim, 34

Lim, Mark, J. S., 86
McCoy, Mike, 132
Malassigné, Pascal, 30
Means, Bridget, 151
Metaxatos, Paul, 97
Moore, Patricia, 226
Muller, Leslie, 144
Murray, James, 202
Naoi, Yukiko, 64
Nelson, Louis, 174
Owens, Kevin, 211
Pellone, Giovanni, 151
Salm, Jaime, 234
Sanz, Victor, 205
Schloss, Andrew, 57
Schmidt, George, 99
Smith, Lisa, 165
Stowell, Davin, 82
Tanaka, Kazuna, 64
Thurston, Steve, 20
Toulis, Tad, 107
Turchi, Mario, 68
Unger, Goetz, 38
Vetter, Craig, 242
Viemeister, Tucker, 89
Vogel, Craig, 23
Wesner, Alecia, 51
Zaccai, Gianfranco, 103
Zogg, Jon, 198